T0171353

TRAVEL
through
EPHESIANS
TRANSFORMING GRACE

THOMAS L. HIEGEL

WESTBOW
PRESS
A DIVISION OF THOMAS NELSON

WestBow Press books may be ordered through booksellers or by contacting:

WestBow Press
A Division of Thomas Nelson
1663 Liberty Drive
Bloomington, IN 47403
www.westbowpress.com
1-(866) 928-1240

Because of the dynamic nature of the Internet, any web addresses or links contained in
this book may have changed since publication and may no longer be valid. The views
expressed in this work are solely those of the author and do not necessarily reflect the
views of the publisher, and the publisher hereby disclaims any responsibility for them.

Any people depicted in stock imagery provided by Thinkstock are models,
and such images are being used for illustrative purposes only.

Certain stock imagery © Thinkstock.

ISBN: 978-1-4497-9944-1 (sc)
ISBN: 978-1-4497-9945-8 (hc)
ISBN: 978-1-4497-9943-4 (e)

Library of Congress Control Number: 2013911508

Printed in the United States of America.

WestBow Press rev. date: 06/28/2013

TABLE OF CONTENTS

PREFACE

T his book is the initial publishing of a series of my *"Travel Through"* expositional study courses. Each book in the series draws from a life-long study of the Scriptures. Many personal notes were written on scraps of paper during study time and as I reviewed various authors' works. If I have utilized thoughts, revelations and insights, without giving credit, I apologize. I have included a list of source materials in attempt to honor their work.

Together we are going to embark upon a personal or group detailed study of the Bible Book of Ephesians. I would suggest using this study side-by-side with a Bible. A study on an entire book of the Bible can be extensive, but extremely uplifting. A verse-by-verse study can be fulfilling and satisfying.

I have taught through the book of Ephesians several times and am sure there is enough revelation and insights to teach every day for a year!

My *"Travel Through"* series is not an exhaustive study of a specific book (I doubt if any commentary is exhaustive). However, the detailed material included will assist the Bible student/ teacher/reader in understanding its content.

Appropriate discussion questions are included throughout which may assist in group sessions or individual study. The questions are clearly identified as **"ASK."** Additional questions and discussions for group consideration can be found at the close of each of the eight Sections (see Outline of Ephesians).

Also available separately, are handout "student outlines" (see author's email address), with appropriate answers to fill-in blanks. These handouts could be used when teaching a group or as a self-help study.

Part One

THE POSITION OF
THE BELIEVER

ONE

Background / Overview

Paul wrote several New Testament books—this one entitled Ephesians. It was first called "The Letter to the Laodiceans," which is what it is referred to by Paul in Colossians 4:16. Later it was named "The Letter to the Ephesians." It was written while Paul was imprisoned in his own home in Rome in AD 62. He loved the people in Ephesus and desired to communicate with them the importance of who they were—part of the body of Christ living in His blessings. Several ancient copies of Scripture do not include the opening words *at Ephesus.* Two translations which I trust and refer to during study, *The [expanded] Bible*[1] and *Rotherham's Emphasized Bible*[2], refer to saints living in Ephesus, and then note the exclusion in manuscripts. It is reasonable to conclude that the epistle was written to the Ephesus believers and intended to be circulated to churches in Asia Minor.

Paul helped establish the church at the city of Ephesus about seven years earlier during his second missionary journey. On his third missionary journey, he returned and stayed at Ephesus for about three years—from the summer of AD 52 until the spring of AD 55.

Some very significant things happened when Paul stayed in Ephesus on that third missionary journey. We review this from a section in the book of Acts:

19:1-7 Paul baptized some followers of John the Baptist. They also received the Holy Spirit.

19:8-10 He taught in the synagogue for three months, then daily in the hall of Tyrannus for two years.

19:11-12 God healed people through Paul using his handkerchief and aprons at times.

19:13-16 Seven sons of a Jewish priest named Sceva tried to cast out evil spirits in the name of the Lord. The demon claimed to know Jesus and Paul but would not obey the sons.

19:17-20 Many who practiced magic were converted. They burned their books (apparently books of magic or evil).

19:21-41 Paul's reputation as a preacher caused a riot. He was accused of an attempt to destroy the temple of Diana.

20:31 Paul lived in Ephesus for three years.

CITY OF EPHESUS

The port city of Ephesus was amazing; we have today much of the footprint of the city. It was the capital of the Roman province of Asia, now extreme western Turkey. At the time of Paul, Ephesus's population approached half a million. We have pictures of the ruins of the main Roman road; a column still standing from the great temple, which seated 25,000; partial walls of several other temples; sections of the three great market places; the steps that led to Domitian's temple, along with Domitian's fountain where his statue would have been. All this allows a partial view of the city in Paul's day.

Ephesus was the center of commerce for Asia, which was completely under Roman control and influence. Being a major seaport, many entered the city from the harbor side. Paul arrived by ship on at least one occasion, so would have walked down the marble street and looked up at the largest stadium in the world. Both the street and stadium ruins can still be viewed today.

Important in our study is the fact that Ephesus was the center of idol worship and occult/magic practices. The great temple dedicated to the Greek goddess Artemis, also known as Diana to the Romans, was a huge 425 x 220 foot building and considered one of the seven wonders of the ancient world. It featured over one hundred outside columns, each fifty-five feet tall. This, along with temple worship in Pergamum and Smyrna, were for worship of the Roman emperor. We still have the complete foundation of it today and know exactly where the idol of Artemis stood.

In this idolatrous city, filled with people who knew nothing about Christianity, Priscilla and Aquila, friends of Paul, planted a Christian church. Paul came back and worked with them to stabilize it. Later, Timothy and John served as pastors of the church.

Today we have the footprint of the Apostle John's home located on a hill just behind and overlooking the Temple of Artemis. I would note that John's home was *above* the Temple. He looked down at the temple and saw people worshipping gods in it. How his heart must have gone out to the people as he saw Roman soldiers take many into the coliseum. John could also look down and see the gladiators in the huge stadium on his right and the huge marketplace on his left. Irenaeus, a church leader during the second century, confirmed that the apostle John lived and ministered in Ephesus during the late first century.

The hill John lived on was on the outskirts of the city, which kept a lot of opposition away. That's why it was a little surprising when the Roman soldiers showed up at his front door and demanded he bow down to a new statue—the statue of the Emperor of Rome, Domitian. He refused to bow so they took him to Rome to stand in front of Domitian. When John again refused to bow or burn incense to the Emperor, tradition tells us that they put him in a pot of boiling oil. He just stepped out of the pot, unharmed.

Ephesians is one of the four prison letters. **ASK:** *Can you name the other three prison letters?*[3]

Since most of Paul's letters were written before any of the other New Testament books, we can conclude that he had only Mark's Gospel when he wrote Ephesians. The Gospels of Matthew and Luke were written shortly after Ephesians. I find it interesting that the Gospel writers had

Paul's writings when they wrote their books, yet included little of his revelation.

The following dates are the *consensus* of up to sixty-seven scholars:

New Testament Book	Year Written	Author
1 Thessalonians	AD 51 early	Paul
2 Thessalonians	AD 51 mid	Paul
Galatians	AD 51 late	Paul
1 Corinthians	AD 55 early	Paul
2 Corinthians	AD 56 early	Paul
Romans	AD 56 late	Paul
Philippians	AD 59 late	Paul
Philemon	AD 60 mid	Paul
Colossians	AD 60 mid	Paul
James	AD 60 late	James
Mark	AD 61 mid	Mark
Ephesians	**AD 61 mid**	**Paul**
1 Timothy	AD 63 late	Paul
Titus	AD 64 early	Paul
1 Peter	AD 64 mid	Peter
Matthew	AD 65 early	Matthew
2 Timothy	AD 65 late	Paul
Luke	AD 66 mid	Luke
Hebrews	AD 67 mid	Unknown
Acts	AD 67 mid	Luke
2 Peter	AD 68 mid	Peter
Jude	AD 71 mid	Jude
John	AD 86 mid	John the Apostle
1 John	AD 89 mid	John the Apostle
2 John	AD 90 early	John the Apostle
3 John	AD 90 early	John the Apostle
Revelation	AD 92 early	John the Apostle

THE BOOK OF EPHESIANS

Let's note some additional information about the book of Ephesians.

This book is quite rich in language and revelation. As we come to different topics and themes, each one of us can learn something.

For example, perhaps you already know some things about *adoption* in Christ, *grace, Paul's mystery, spiritual warfare,* or *God's armor.*

You may know about your old life before knowing Christ and your new life in Him as a believer. We all can further learn from Paul's teachings, which we will review. Our goal is to grow in knowledge and wisdom in spiritual matters.

Each one of us can mature as we receive Paul's teachings into our spirit. Whether you are in church, on the way home from church, visiting friends, or most importantly, in your home, these truths should be at the center of your life. After all, a believer's life is 24/7.

I've always taught that if the teachings of Paul are only head knowledge, or if they are lived and expressed only in church and not applied in your home and daily life, then one may be lacking spiritual maturity. Okay? Do you still love me? Ephesians is going to be fun!

Armitage Robinson called Ephesians "the crown of Saint Paul's writings."[4]

Sir Francis Bacon once wrote, "Some books are to be tasted, others to be swallowed, and some few to be chewed and digested."[5]

We are going to do some chewing, and, hopefully, digest many thoughts from the book of Ephesians.

Ephesians is the pinnacle of Paul's writings. I think of it as the Holy of Holies for each of us. John Mackay called it "the greatest . . . maturest . . . . and for our time the most relevant" of Paul's writings. It presents the basic doctrines of Christianity clearly and practically. This is why we study Ephesians.

ASK: The most frequently used phrase in the book is only two words— *Can you guess what the two words are?*[6]

This point is made clear as we review the emphasis of the two words. They emphasize the heart of Paul's message. If you are *in Christ,* you have everything! You are not lacking anything for a blessed life. For example Christians are:

Saints *IN Christ* (1:1)
Blessed *IN Christ* (1:3)
Chosen *IN Him* (1:4)
Lavished with love *IN Christ* (1:6)
Redeemed and forgiven *IN Christ* (1:7)
Glorified *IN Christ* (1:12-13)
Have Faith *IN Christ* (1:15)
Wisdom *IN Him* (1:17)
Hope *IN Christ* (1:18)
Power *IN Christ* (1:19-20)
Made alive *IN Christ* (2:5-6)
Created *IN Christ* (2:10)
Brought near to God *IN Christ* (2:13)
Growing *IN Christ* (2:21)
Built *IN Christ* (2:22)

That is just in the first two chapters! We will look at this in detail in Paul's introduction to his letter.

You can always know that you are not alone. You are not in a battle without weapons to win; you are a part of a team. You and the family of God have teamwork. Call on God and His family during your time of need.

Let us think a little more on this. As a Christian, you are part of the family of God, which makes you royalty.

That makes you a prince or princess of the King of the universe. Ephesians tells us who we are. For now, consider the following:

Once you are *in Christ,*

You have a future inheritance *in* Him (Ephesians 1:11, 12)
You live *in* His power (1:19, 20)
You died to sin, *with* Him (2:6)
You live *with* Him in life (2:10, 11)

In later lessons, we will list additional thoughts concerning who you are because of new life.

Paul will tell us in vv. 4-5 in cp. 1 of Ephesians that every Christian is adopted into God's family. You are loved into His own family.

Adoption by God is one of the most life-changing truths found in the Scriptures. In Paul's day, an adopted child had all the rights, and privileges of a natural born son or daughter.

The Roman judicial system recognized an adopted child as a new person, with a fresh, clean start. That child was given a new name and was born-again—all legal procedures of Rome. All former debts and obligations were cancelled, wiped out. Paul's audience understood the meaning of being adopted.

May I suggest that you stop at this point and reflect on who you are *in Christ*? During the next few days, keep in mind who you are, and where you are . . . . *in Christ.*

As we edge further into the background of Ephesians, allow me to present an overview of this great book. Here are listed five observations of our inheritance as believers in Christ. We will address most of these observations somewhere in Ephesians—several are in cp. 1. However, as we begin the text, we need to have this knowledge in our heads and in our hearts.

First observation: When we become a part of God's family, *we get many brothers and sisters.* I like that. I can tell you this that whenever I stand in front of a group of Christians to teach, I look out and see my brothers, sisters. Usually my opening comments will refer to my brothers and sisters in Christ. Years ago, we called each other brother or sister, which is certainly appropriate.

So, let's remember this when we meet with our God-family on Sundays, because we will be with them throughout eternity.

Second observation: *Each of us has a unique and intimate relationship* with our Father. You can call Him "daddy," it is ok. The Bible confirms this relationship. The word *abba* in Mark 14:36, Romans 8:15 and Galatians 4:6, has an Aramaic origin-meaning father. The Father loves His children. Do you realize that whenever He wants to see you, all He has to do is look in the palm of His hand! (Isaiah 49:2 *In the shadow of His hand He has concealed Me*)

Third observation: *Every believer is an heir with Jesus to everything that God owns.* Hello! We will see this heritage when we study about being sealed by the Holy Spirit.

> Just a side observation—during the first century, an adopted son was given his father's ring. You may know how the story goes. The son used the ring to prove his authority. We will look more at that later, but I just want you to know ahead of time that you have a seal of God.

Fourth observation: *Every believer has a position that will continue into eternity.* It cannot be stolen from you, it is guaranteed. Even better, no angel or any created being will share your individuality of a child of God. (I had better make it clear—no misunderstandings—I did not say you could not walk away from your position in Christ).

Fifth observation: *Every believer will rule the nations with Christ* during the 1000-year period when Christ returns with His church. We could continue on and on in this point and say every Christian will have a new body and a home in heaven. This is all a part of your wonderful future with Christ.

OUTLINE OF THE BOOK OF EPHESIANS								
AREAS OF STUDY	**THE POSITION OF THE BELIEVER** 1:1 — 3:21				**THE PRACTICE OF THE BELIEVER** 4:1 — 6:24			
Sections	The Believer's Riches In Christ	The Believer's Enlightenment	The Believer's Victory	The Believer's Maturity	Unity of Believers	Morality of Believers	Life at Home and Work for the Believer	Warfare and the Believer
Verses	1:1-1:14	1:15-1:23	2:1-2:22	3:1-3:21	4:1-4:16	4:17-5:20	5:21-6:9	6:10-6:24
Topics	Doctrinal				Practical			
	Who the Believer is				What the Believer Does			

Keys to Ephesians:

Key verses: *Ephesians 4:1-3*

¹ I THEREFORE, the prisoner for the Lord, appeal to and beg you to walk (lead a life) worthy of the [divine] calling to which you have been called [with behavior that is a credit to the summons to God's service,

² Living as becomes you] with complete lowliness of mind (humility) and meekness (unselfishness, gentleness, mildness), with patience, bearing with one another and making allowances because you love one another.

³ Be eager and strive earnestly to guard and keep the harmony and oneness of [and produced by] the Spirit in the binding power of peace.

Key words: *In Christ, walk, blessing, mystery, power*
Key persons: *Saints*

TWO

In Christ

The first Section of our study (see the Outline) will reflect on Ephesians 1:1-14. The main title: **The Believer's Riches In Christ.** Each chapter of the study will have a sub-title, to assist in remembering the specific topic. The first one is being *"In Christ."*

> *[1] PAUL, AN apostle (special messenger) of Christ Jesus (the Messiah), by the divine will (the purpose and the choice of God) to the saints (the consecrated, set-apart ones) at Ephesus who are also faithful and loyal and steadfast in Christ Jesus.*

PAUL, AN apostle of Christ Jesus

This is literally Paul's only claim.

Not a birthright
Not his position or reputation *made* him Christ's Apostle.

Paul did not claim his superior intellect made him an apostle. His being a Hebrew of the Hebrews was not his claim of authority. His memorizing The Law, which he certainly did, did not give him a right to author this book. He had many natural and positional qualifications—none of which qualified him for apostleship.

PAUL, AN apostle of Christ Jesus. This is Paul's only claim. What a great statement. Don't you want to acknowledge something similar? Perhaps you would say, *"I am a believer of Christ, totally belonging to Jesus"* or *"My claim is being in Christ."* All I have is His, any ability, any gifting, any good characteristics, great or small—are His. I place myself in His care. That's Paul's attitude here when he writes **PAUL, AN apostle of Christ Jesus.**

The name Paul means "small." Paul was his Roman name; his Jewish name had been Saul. Moreover, he probably *was* small in physical stature, but he was a giant in spiritual influence.

God does not view physical appearance as being of prime importance. Jesus did not call Saul because of his physical appearance. Aren't you glad that your physical appearance has nothing to do with your acceptance to Christ? I know that I am thankful for that! God looks at the heart, not the physical appearance.

"Apostle" means, "sent one," however, Paul uses the word in a unique way. He used it in a distinctive way, almost creating a new word. (We will see more of these unique words later).

Paul is saying that he was handpicked, commissioned by Christ, to a specific mission: To preach the gospel to the Gentiles and teach the great truth concerning the Church. This is his new definition of "apostle of Jesus Christ."

Saul, a Jew of Tarsus, became Paul, the apostle to the Gentiles. Transformation!

This was a confusing time for the Jew, and because of this confusion, Matthew was later instructed by God to write a gospel to them.

During the approximate same time, Luke wrote a letter to the Gentiles, to help *them* understand the new message Paul was teaching. The Jews had expected a Kingdom—one in which they would serve as rulers. Paul's revelation of the mystery was that Jew and Gentile, *anyone* who accepted Jesus, would be engrafted into this vine, forming one body, the true church. *Stay* in the vine and you have your life support.

During the study of the book of Ephesians, keep in mind that it was written by this **apostle of Christ**. Paul was not some private individual venting his personal opinions, nor a gifted teacher, or the church's greatest missionary; he was an **apostle of Christ.**

Note in v. 1, this person writing this book is not some unknown historian. This book was written under the authority of Christ. Remember that fact as you travel through this letter written to the Ephesus believers. Paul states at the beginning of the book that it is written **by the divine will of God.**

Paul stated in his opening remarks of Ephesians:

"I *am who I am* because of Christ"

"I *do what I do* because of Christ"

SAINTS

Next, Paul writes **"to the saints."** This letter was not written to the lost, but rather to the found, and I love this fact.

When Paul called the believers at Ephesus "saints," it was nothing special. The important emphasis was their identification as believers, in Christ. In fact, there was no other requirement for them to be called **saints**, other than to believe in the One who met Paul during that Damascene Road experience. The word *saint* comes from the Greek word *hajiois,* meaning "pure, morally blameless, consecrated" and it is used sixty-two times in the Bible. Saint never refers to someone who has earned that title. Saint identifies the person, or item, called *hajios* as set apart from others. A Christian is a "saint" because he or her has been cleansed of his/her sins through Jesus' death, and considered by God to be pure and acceptable. Paul's primary goal in this letter to believers is to help them learn how to live in their spiritual role as saints. The original Greek word translated "saint" in English means "one who is set apart for God's use."

Charles R. Swindoll wrote, "Let me suggest that we not think of saints as some exceptionally pious, almost superhuman group of people, but as real people like you and me, thoroughly human, garden-variety, sinful people **saved** by the **grace** of God."[7]

I believe that no word in the New Testament has been more mistreated than the word "saint."

Nine times in his letter to the Ephesians, Paul addressed his readers as saints or believers (1:1, 15, 18; 2:19; 3:8, 18; 4:12; 5:3; 6:18)—at least once in every chapter.

I want to identify with these saints! Alive—not dead. In light—not darkness. Adopted—not orphaned. Chosen—not left out.

The book of Ephesians is directed to believers. Since Paul's words **at Ephesus** in the first chapter and verse are not found in many manuscripts, we could understand that the book may have been meant for circulation to many churches in addition to Ephesus. Seven churches (listed in Revelation cp. 1) were located within a few miles of each other. Ephesians is identifying who you are, describing you as one of the saints, and it was not written to the "religious ones" but rather to the saved! Paul's writings clearly declare that anyone who believes in Christ is a saint. Therefore, it is biblical to declare, *"I am a saint."* We usually don't say it that way, but I am making it clear, this letter is for each one of us today.

I want to know who I am, and what I possess, don't you? Certainly one of the purposes of this course is to establish who you are and what you possess. Paul's writing of Ephesians serve as a reminder of your position as a believer in Christ.

You could be made a president or chief officer of a college, bank or mega company—

- and do nothing
- be a failure
- make no decisions
- have no respect
- be in poverty—if you did not know what the position included.

However, when that president or officer steps in to his position and stands in his office, and learns who he is—he then has authority to use all the available benefits that are his. He now has security, he now has confidence, and he is in the position of being an active believer.

God says to the Ephesians readers and to each of us, *"here my child . . . . .this is your identity, your position; stand in your rights!"*

Notice the first thing Paul writes about these saints and about us—We have three—defining characteristics, **"who are also _faithful_ and _loyal_** *and <u>steadfast</u> in Christ Jesus."* The Amplified Bible (AMP) translation lists three similar words describing our solid position.

These words have a couple of meanings all related to *faithful*: First they can mean, "exercising faith" (full of faith and using it to call things that be not as though they are) *faith-full*. Second, they could mean "to continue in faith", (going on, walking through the waters of difficulties, the rivers of mounting problems that are faced and the awful fires of life that Isaiah 43 explains). Ephesians 1 probably carries both meanings. The Ephesians had believed in Christ for the forgiveness of their sins, and *now* they were continuing to rely on God and grow in Him. What a lesson for each of us. Believe in Him by faith—then live a life of continual faith.

BELIEVERS ARE IN CHRIST

Notice the wonderful theme Paul develops in his letters—it's actually developed in the first four letters of the New Testament, (Romans, 1 & 2 Corinthians and Galatians) previously written by Paul. And, he continues the same doctrine here in Ephesians.

Notice that in the first verse he writes, *in Christ Jesus.* You can be IN many things, and not in Christ. Isn't that right? **ASK:** *What are some things you could you be in, and not be in Christ?*

- You can be IN church
- IN religion, or some great teaching or philosophy
- You may join a fraternity or local service club
- You might be IN your vocation or even a vacation
- Perhaps you are IN relatives or relationships
- Or in friends or Pastors—and never be IN Jesus

There is probably nothing wrong with being into these activities or persons, but the believer is *in Christ*. Moreover, you are to be faithful in that knowledge. Know that you are In Christ. You are not in the world or worldly things.

I love this term "In Christ" or "In the Lord," or "In Him." It's Paul's 'thing' and found at least 160 times in Paul's Epistles—36 times in Ephesians.

"In Christ" means that the believer is united with Jesus through a personal relationship. The character and purposes of Christ are now yours. This relationship with Christ is the believer's new environment. Being "*in Christ*" means each of us as brothers and sisters are constantly aware of our Lord's presence and companionship. No longer is your life your own. Because Christ lives in you, all the activities and purposes of life are viewed as Christ living in you.

ASK: *Would Christ do what I am doing?* Would He go where I go, look at what I am looking at, say what I said? Your personal unity and walk with Christ is the most important thing in the Christian life. Realize that this union with Christ comes as a gift of God through faith.

Let us go further into this phrase, "in Christ." There is no deeper word in all of Scripture than this tiny word *in*.

- God is IN all
- He dwells IN Christ
- Christ lives IN God
- We are IN Christ and Christ is IN us.

Our life is taken up *into* His. His life is received into ours. Words cannot express the thought "we are in Him and He is in us." It reminds me of the great fifteenth chapter of John concerning the vine (Christ) and branches (believers). The idea of "grafting" is a theme of our life. As branches, we grow down into the stem of the vine. The stem grows up into the branch. The sap (Holy Spirit) then flows into each branch in producing life of fruit.

I hope you receive what Paul meant concerning your acceptance of Christ—*it's deep, it's a connection, and it's being joined IN Jesus.*

God does not see you *in Adam* any longer—now He sees you *in Christ,* clothed in Christ's acceptance.

THREE

The Believer's Blessings I

We continue in Ephesians 1

²May grace (God's unmerited favor) and spiritual peace [which means peace with God and harmony, unity, and undisturbedness] be yours from God our Father and from the Lord Jesus Christ.

Every letter of Paul's begins with those same words, **grace and peace.** He adds **mercy** to his letters to the preachers, Timothy and Titus, and for a good reason. Let's camp on these two words, **grace and peace**.

Paul recognized the important benefits Christians share in by beginning his letter by saying in effect, *"Christians, you have grace and peace because you are believers in Jesus."* There could not have been a better welcoming statement spoken to those about to read his letter.

> "Grace" is virtually the first and last word of every epistle of Paul. The repetition of Paul using grace declares the importance God has placed on His grace to those in Jesus.

The single principle, which revolved around all of Paul's teachings, was grace. Grace produces the transformation from "old" to "new" which is what Paul preached. It removes your old, filthy *garments of sin*, replaces them with new clean "white as snow" *garments of grace*.

Every one of Paul's letters *begins* with grace, and inside every letter, he *imparted* grace.

> [2] *May grace and spiritual peace.*

Grace and Peace are the love twins of God's nature that become yours because you are **IN** Christ.

We will not go into depth on this, but know: **Grace** is God's willingness to get involved with you on a personal basis—*and* make available to you all that He is—all of His identity—all His life, even though *in yourself*, you do not deserve any of it. However, *in Christ*—you receive it all!

Paul uses grace twelve times in Ephesians; always referring to "the kindness of God toward undeserving people." We are to extend this same grace to others.

Grace means accepting ourselves and others' failures, shortcomings, mistakes, and accepting it all. Grace forgives—and goes on.

ASK: *Just how do you forgive and go on?*

This would be a good place to explain three terms:

> **Justice** is receiving what we deserve.
> **Mercy** is being spared from what we deserve.
> **Grace** is being given what we do not deserve.

Then there is the *peace* that Paul links to *grace.* Peace is being free from all fear, having all the necessary good and well-being in every situation and in all things. Not very natural, is it?

It is a spirit of rest in all the circumstances of life. You actually, enter the "rest" of peace. Hebrews 4:1 assures us ***THEREFORE, WHILE the promise of entering His rest still holds and is offered [today].***

I love the following story of a contest. Each artist was asked to paint his/her concept of peace. One artist painted a quiet brook, another painted two warriors shaking hands while the third artist painted peace by showing a lion and lamb together. The winner though, painted a wind and rainstorm with lightning flashing all around. Far out on the tip of a tree branch was a mother bird hovering over her tiny baby—with confidence and assurance. Peace!

> Peace **WITH** God comes at salvation, but peace **OF** God is needed. This is received by faith, and matured into your life.

Notice the order of grace and peace, because it is always the same way. *Grace* of God has to come, before the *peace* of God.

If you know and respect God's grace, peace will be close behind. Peace is one of the products of grace. I used to illustrate this to a group of people by having two volunteers join me on the platform. One I would name "Grace," the other "Peace." As Grace would walk forward, Peace was instructed to be close behind. *Grace* would run, *Peace* would be right behind. Each of us was saved by the grace of God, and His peace is close behind. Believe *in* it and walk *with* it.

> [3] *May blessing (praise, laudation, and eulogy) be to the God and Father of our Lord Jesus Christ (the Messiah) Who has blessed us in Christ with every spiritual (given by the Holy Spirit) blessing in the heavenly realm!*

Paul has completed his normal greeting to the readers with grace and peace upon them. He mentioned the *source* of our blessings, which is God our Father. Even though God created every person ever born, that does not mean He is everyone's spiritual Father. Only those who have received Jesus into their hearts can actually claim God as their Father. Jesus named another spiritual "father," the devil. Everyone has one of two spiritual fathers: God or Satan (the devil).

Now Paul moves into the *scope* of those blessings as he is writing to believers, using his familiar phrase, *"in Christ."*

Paul has told us that when we are *in Christ*, we have an overflowing number of wonderful benefits, or blessings, to enjoy. In the next few verses, he names many of them, even though they are not the complete list. Later in this letter and in his other letters he will list additional benefits or blessings. In the passage we are studying, Paul seems to delight in encouraging believers with a list of spiritual "rights" they have.

A LONG SENTENCE

Verses 3-14 are a single sentence in the Greek, which Paul used, and it is the very heart of his letter. I interpret this entire paragraph as Paul's emphasis on encouragement and building the self-confidence to those who read this letter. How we see and feel about ourselves builds *our* confidence level. So, Paul uses twelve verses to write that single sentence. Verse 3 begins this very long sentence, one of several extended sentences Paul uses in the letter. In the Greek, there are no periods at the end of any verses between 3 and 14. I find at least nine blessings mentioned in this sentence, to build confidence for every believer. That is a lot of blessing for each of us. The sentence is long and complicated, because it represents a song of praise as Paul's mind goes on and on, as the many blessings from God seem to pass before his spiritual eyes.

Paul breaks into praise in these next few verses as he writes [3] *May blessing be to the God and Father of our Lord Jesus Christ Who has blessed us in Christ with every spiritual blessing*

> God has blessed us . . . . He chose each one of us, [4] "*before the foundation of the world.*"

He knew us before we knew Him; loved us before we had the ability to love back; accepted us in Christ even when our sin blocked us from accepting ourselves.

He expounds on nine **Blessings of the Believer** in these twelve verses. These blessings are part of the grace that transforms us—nine blessings which we must know. Some of these you may already know and are walking in them. You may need to understand and *begin* to walk in some others. They are part of the body of riches which we are given when we accept Jesus.

These nine blessings are what identify you and me—set us apart. Moreover, if we teach only on these blessings, and go no further in Ephesians, and learn to walk in these nine benefits, we will have accomplished enough for this entire book.

Every day, in these twelve verses, you can read what you have in your spiritual bank account. You may have never *drawn* on your account, or only tapped a small amount of it.

These nine blessings identify your position in Christ.

When I was drafted into the Army, I was told who I was and my identity made quite clear to me from the first day.

- I was given a number
- My head was shaved
- I was given green clothing to wear
- I was shouted at for every move
- I knew who I was, in *this* Army
- I was identified.

Christ says when you come into the army and family of God—you are identified—changed—and you learn your full identity.

ASK: *What does your transformation look like?*

Notice as we continue that, all the fullness of God is behind these nine blessings. The Trinity has worked together to tell us what we have. From Paul's view, he draws from the past, present and future to emphasize the Godhead at work. God the Father acted in eternity past, Jesus the Son living in us now, and the Holy Spirit guaranteeing our future.

> The **Father** initiated three of them,
> The **Son** implemented four,
> The **Holy Spirit** empowers two.

Another way to summarize these blessings is to realize that they all are part of our redemption.

> The **Father** planned our redemption
> The **Son** paid the price to secure our redemption
> And the **Spirit** applies them all to us

OUR SPIRITUAL BLESSINGS

First, in verse 3 we see a praise for *all nine* blessings **Who has blessed us in Christ with every spiritual blessing.** Perhaps this is a good place for each one of us to begin: Say it *"thank you Lord for all you have done."*

Paul begins with giving glory to our Father and with acknowledgement to the fullness of our Savior, the Son.

He refers to **our Lord Jesus Christ.** This is the full title of our Lord, a title that is used by Paul at least fifty times, with six times in Ephesians.

> As our **Lord,** He has full rights to all we are and all we have. We are not our own.

> As our **Jesus**, He is our Savior from sin. He paid the ransom. You and I can pay no price or do any work, to qualify us for life in Him.

> Then, as our **Christ**, He is divinely anointed as Prophet, Priest and King. This is the full title as well as description of the person of Jesus.

So, feast on the blessings that identify each of us who is *in Christ:*

> **Blessing #1:** WRITE IT DOWN (writing it down will help you learn and remember it): ***I HAVE ALL THE BLESSINGS OF THE SPIRIT.*** That is how this could be translated. *This* one makes possible all nine of these blessings.

It is not just all spiritual blessings; it is all the blessings of the Spirit. These are all the blessings that the Spirit (capital S) has empowered!

Because you are *in* Jesus, every blessing given by the Holy Spirit—is yours. The Holy Spirit is mentioned many times in this letter, because He is the One who channels God's blessings to us. However wait, it gets better!

> ***Blessing*** means "to benefit, to prosper, and to give contentment." The word appears hundreds of times in the Bible.

Here, Paul uses it in the past tense. **Who has blessed us.** It is a done deal.

He refers to *"heavenly places"* meaning they came from above, not earthly, not temporal. Secured *in* heaven, and then given to each of us *on* earth.

Now think on this: What are these blessings given by the Holy Spirit?

They are best summarized in 2 Peter 1:21 *For prophecy never had its origin in the will of man, but men spoke from God as they were carried along by the Holy Spirit.*

Every promise was a Spirit-given blessing, and most of them were given to every believer! Yes there were some given specifically to a person for that time, but most were universal and unending to those *"who are faithful IN Christ Jesus."* God, His Word, and His character never change**.** He *is* today the same in character as He *was* in the past.

> **Blessing #2** is [4] *Even as [in His love] He chose us [actually picked us out for Himself as His own] in Christ before the foundation of the world, that we should be holy (consecrated and set apart for Him) and blameless in His sight, even above reproach, before Him in love.*

Write down blessing #2: *GOD CHOSE ME*

Oh, it is wonderful to be chosen!

You can stand tall and know you are chosen! You may think people do not like you for some reason, or maybe someone does not accept you. Nevertheless, thank God, you are chosen and accepted in Christ.

I remember as a young boy learning to play football in the neighborhood, and being the last one chosen. The reason was not important. I just knew I wasn't chosen—until only one was left—me. What a "bummer". Actually I was not *chosen* at all—I was the leftover.

This is the amazing doctrine many call "election." This doctrine is misunderstood by many and confusing to others. Also, many people will not go near it. Some mistakenly say that the doctrine teaches that God elects one, and rejects another. H. A. Ironside: "There is no such thing taught in the Word of God as predestination to eternal condemnation.

If men are lost, they are lost because they do not come to Christ. When men do come to Christ, they learn the wonderful secret that God has foreknown it all from eternity."[8]

Many books have been written on this verse, which confirms that it is much more than a benefit or blessing, it is indeed a doctrine.

Always realize that God loves every person ever born. He has elected to accept into His family any person accepting His Son. God does not do the choosing of the specific individual, it is the individual who makes a choice.

An election is always *unto* something. God elected us *in Christ* to be holy and without blame. He sees you, He see me, without sin, blameless, redeemed. You are hidden in His Son and He looks at His Son. He elected to do it that way, not wanting anyone to be lost, (2 Peter 3:9) but allowing everyone to choose Christ. He *chose* a human being *to choose* Christ. Always know that salvation comes from the Lord. Paul makes it clear in these verses as he teaches us that God **chose** (v. 4), **foreordained**(v. 5), **freely bestowed** (v. 6), **redeemed** (v. 7), **lavished** (v. 8), **made known His will** (v. 9), **planned** (v. 10), and **marked** us with a seal of the Spirit (v. 13).

This would be a good place to pause. Reflect for a few days on the realization, that God has blessed every one of His children with many blessings. Just walk the next few days knowing He loves you and wants to be big in your daily life.

Always know you were not a surprise to God. You were not an accident or mistake or some afterthought. God knew you before you were conceived in mother's womb.

FOUR

The Believer's Blessings II

I remember a cartoon that was quite humorous. A lawyer was reading a client's last will and testament to a group of greedy relatives; the caption read: "I, John Jones, being of sound mind and body, have spent it all!" The relatives must have gasped in shock and disappointment.

When Jesus Christ wrote *His* last will and testament, He made it possible for each one of us to share His spiritual riches. These nine blessings are part of those riches.

Jesus did not *spend* it all. Jesus Christ *paid* it all. What we are seeing in these early verses of Ephesians is that this was not only for our salvation. You and I have a whole lot more!

Jesus *wrote* us into His will, and then *He died* so that His will would be carried out. Then He arose in order that He might become the heavenly Advocate (lawyer) to make sure the terms of the will are correctly followed! So in this long sentence (a reminder that vv. 3—14 are one sentence in the Greek), Paul named just a few of the blessings that make up our spiritual wealth. Blessing #1 was *"I have all the blessings of the Holy Spirit."* Blessing #2 was *"God Chose Me."*

Let's read vv. 5-6, **Blessing #3** [5] *For He foreordained us (destined us, planned in love for us) to be adopted (revealed) <u>as His own children</u> through Jesus Christ, in accordance with the purpose of His will [because it pleased Him and was His kind intent]—6 [So that we might be] to the praise*

and the commendation of His glorious grace (favor and mercy), which He so freely bestowed on us in the Beloved.
(Underline added for emphasis)

Write down blessing #3 *GOD ADOPTED ME!*

Here we face that misunderstood word *foreordained.* Some translations call it "predestined." *Foreordained* is the Greek word *proorizo* which means "to mark out ahead of time," and is found six times in the New Testament: Acts 4:28, Romans 8:29-30, 1 Corinthians 2:7, and Ephesians 1:5, 11.

Sometimes the words, election and predestination, are used in the same sentence. However, we *do* need to understand the difference between election and predestination. This word, (the AMP *foreordained* gives a much better understanding than predestined) is used in the Bible, to express what God has *determined* for His people. He predetermined beforehand, to do some things *for His Children*. He did not predestine any human being to hell. This word refers only to God's people.

The word "election" is mentioned in the previous (second) blessing. Election refers to *people;* God chose to accept any person who would accept Christ (election). "Foreordained," this third blessing is referring to a *purpose* or *event* God had in mind, not a people. This must be understood.

For example the events connected with the crucifixion of Christ were foreordained (Acts 4:25-28). God has foreordained our adoption (with it comes all His blessings) as well as our future inheritance of a glorified body. (Ephesians 1:11)

So, Election=People
Predestination=Purpose (event)

The Greek implies that God "marked out beforehand" some benefits for saved people.

Paul's audience understood the Roman law. Roman law said adopted children were to enjoy the same rights as natural children. There is little difference today. Realize the terminology used in these two blessings: Paul is saying God elected us by His Grace, and has now legally ordained an adoption for us to be His sons.

You are not *in* His family by adoption. You are in the family by a new birth—a regeneration, an election by a person. *Adoption* is the act of God placing you into a legal position to claim your inheritance.

Then Paul seems to be caught up with sort of an exclamation; he seems to take a deep breath, a holy 'gasp' at the glories of the grace that allowed for that election and allowed for the adoption.

> [6] *He so freely bestowed . . . . on us*

We are the recipients of His grace; we receive what He freely did. Of course, Jesus is the channel of God's grace; ***in the Beloved*** as v. 6 ends.

> Then **Blessing #4** is [7a] ***In Him we have redemption (deliverance and salvation) through His blood.*** We just looked at **God's** part of blessing you,

He *chose* you and He *adopted* you—that was the Father's decision. Now we look at Christ's part.

> Write down blessing #4 ***CHRIST REDEEMED ME.*** That's good news.

I teach a course, *Advanced Foundations For A Living Faith*[9], which details redemption and other foundations of our Christian life. Our foundation as believers must be built on the solid teachings of Scripture.

To *redeem* means, "to purchase and set free by paying a price." There were sixty million slaves in the Roman Empire; many of them were bought and sold like pieces of clothing. The law allowed a man to purchase a slave and set him/her free, and is exactly what Jesus did for us.

Redemption is the *most glorious* work of God. It is greater than His work of creation. Think about that. The word *redemption* occurs three times in Paul's letter to the Ephesians (1:7, 14; 4:30) and is essential to Christianity. I love to think of Jesus as my "Redeemer." Matthew 20:28 makes it clear, ***Just as the Son of Man came not to be waited on but to serve, and to give His life as a ransom for many [the price paid to set them free].***

Anytime you buy something, you have in a sense redeemed it. You have paid a price for that item to become yours. It is now your possession and you can do with it, as you like. In the same way, God "bought" us from the possession of Satan and death with the high cost of Jesus' blood on the cross. After we are purchased, or "redeemed," we belong to God, and He can do anything He wants with us.

He spoke a Word . . . . and worlds were formed, but it cost Him the life of His Son to redeem the same world! You and I were stolen away by a spirit system of this world and made slaves to an enemy; *now* you and I can come back. Isn't that a great reality?

Your redemption was paid in full, not by paying silver or gold but by the precious blood of Jesus Christ offered one time, and for all.

Notice in v. 7, it was **In Him**. Our Lord Jesus is the Redeemer. What a blessing to write down to remind us: **I Have Been Redeemed.**

> **Blessing #5** is in the latter part of v. 7 *the remission (forgiveness) of our offenses (shortcomings and trespasses).*

Write down blessing #5: ***CHRIST HAS FORGIVEN ME.***

Isn't *that* good news? Some of you can *really* shout about this one! Christ no longer considers any of our transgressions, past or present. God sees me, once I am in Christ, with no record of a past. Psalm 103:12 *"As far as the east is from the west, so far has He removed our transgressions from us."*

Christ has no record of our past sins. No past! They are not in any memory bank in heaven. Those "hard drives" of storage are inexhaustible.

The Greek word for *forgive* means "to carry away." This reminds us of the ritual on the Jewish Day of Atonement, when the high priest sent the scapegoat into the wilderness (Leviticus 16:22). First, the priest killed one of the two goats and sprinkled its blood before God on the mercy seat. Then he confessed Israel's sins over the live goat, and had the goat taken into the wilderness to be lost forever.

Christ died to carry away our sins so they might never again be seen (Psalm 103:12; John 1:29). No written accusation stands against us, because our sins have been taken away!

Notice again ⁷*the remission (forgiveness) of our offenses.* Forgiveness is not the same as redemption—forgiveness is one of the *benefits* of redemption—it is the fruit of redemption. Because of God's plan of redemption, you and I have free choice to accept forgiveness.

Now this may be heavy, but realize—we no longer, as children of God, have a sin problem on this earth! It was dealt with above the earth on a hill, set aside and nailed to a tree, lifted up and eradicated in a pit far below.

The believer only has one problem. It is not sin, it is not failure; neither of those.

The believer's only problem is—*choosing,* making a decision. We will always have that problem; sin and its results are around us every day.

No longer is God judging this world according to all the sin that it is doing.

I like 1 John 2:2 *And He [that same Jesus Himself] is the propitiation (the atoning sacrifice) for our sins, and not for ours alone but also for [the sins of] the whole world.*

And Jesus said in John 16, I'll send back the Holy Spirit of God to tell the world of sin (v. 8)—and that sin is *because they do not believe in Me* (v. 9 NASU).

It's good news to know **I am Redeemed** *and* **Forgiven**!

The remainder of verse 7 in Ephesians 1 says *in accordance with the riches and the generosity of His gracious favor.*

There is the Father's transforming grace again. Paul used another of his unique words *riches* to ascribe value to this grace. We owe our lives, present and eternal to the riches of God's grace.

This grace was not simply given. Verse 8 finishes this, which *He lavished upon us*, generously showered on us *wisdom and understanding* of it all.

When God gives, He gives abundantly and extravagantly.

> **Blessing #6**, let's read it in vv. 9-10. *Making known to us the mystery (secret) of His will (of His plan, of His purpose). [And it is this:] In accordance with His good pleasure (His merciful intention) which He had previously purposed and set forth in Him,* ¹⁰ *[He planned] for the maturity of the times and the climax of the ages to unify all things and head*

**them up and consummate them in Christ, [both] things in
heaven and things on the earth.**

So write down *this* very good news: **CHRIST HAS REVEALED
GOD'S ETERNAL PLAN TO ME.** We have this blessing: To
know His plan.

Ephesians has much to say about God's plan for His people, a plan
that was not fully understood in Paul's day. His plan would unite Jew and
Gentile into one unified body, His Church. That was the mystery.

This word *mystery* has nothing to do with things "eerie." It means a
"sacred secret, once hidden but now revealed to God's people." This is one of
our benefits. As His children, we are able to share in the secret that God
will one day unite everything in Christ.

This world has been in a mess:

First, man was *separated from God* (Genesis 3).

Then *man* was separated *from man*, when Cain killed Abel (Genesis 4).
People *tried* to maintain a unity by building the Tower of Babel (Genesis
11), but God judged them and scattered them across the earth.

Today, sin is tearing everything apart, but in Christ, God will gather
everything together in the culmination of the ages. Today, we are a part
of this great eternal program.

Every person *in Christ*—Jew or Gentile, black, yellow, red, brown or
white will be gathered together *with* Jesus. That is the goal. That is the
revelation shown to Paul. He was given the knowledge to see a mystery
revealed.

There are some, already *in* heaven—you may know someone there. I
do. That will be some reunion! This knowledge is our blessing. This is such
a comfort to believers.

All of those in heaven, and all of those on earth *in Christ*, in a
"twinkle" of an eye, will be together in Christ with God!

Also, notice the words *"the climax of the ages to unify all things
and head them up."*

This is interesting terminology in the Greek. It is used for adding up
a column of figures.

In our day, we might refer in this world of confusion as 'things are just not adding up" or "this isn't making sense." Believers can look ahead to the time when everything will make sense, under Christ.

Christ is telling us "it's all going to add up." There is a second coming of Christ to earth, ushering in the Millennium.

Concluding in v. 10: God's plan is to ***head them up*** in Christ. God will set up Christ to head up all things heavenly and earthly in the new Kingdom.

FIVE

The Believer's Blessings III

We continue with the last three of the benefits that everyone has "in Christ."

We've seen that—#1 each one of us has **All the Blessings of the Holy Spirit;** we know that each one of us was #2 **Chosen, #3 Adopted, #4 Forgiven and #5 Redeemed.** We know, **#6** that we have been given the knowledge that **God has a plan** to place all *His Children,* whether Jew or Gentile, into a single family—and head everything up in Christ.

> **Blessing #7** is in vv. 11-12. *In Him we also were made [God's] heritage and we obtained an inheritance; for we had been foreordained (chosen and appointed beforehand) in accordance with His purpose, Who works out everything in agreement with the counsel and design of His [own] will,* [12] *So that we who first hoped in Christ [who first put our confidence in Him have been destined and appointed to] live for the praise of His glory*

> More good news to write down (I hope you are writing each of these down. They will encourage you as you review them): ***CHRIST HAS MADE US AN INHERITANCE***

I like the way Paul weaves in a "mystery" here, which was revealed to him by the Holy Spirit. Paul will discuss this mystery later in his letter, no longer referring to something unknown, and no longer referring to a separation between God's people. Note how Paul includes all believers in these blessings, even before explaining the mystery. Paul's words, *In Him we also*, and *we who first hoped in Christ,* along with earlier words such as *has blessed us, He chose us, In Him we,* and *He lavished upon us*, are all referring to the Church.

In v. 11, the word, *foreordained,* refers to all believers receiving an inheritance. An inheritance is received because of a *relationship* with someone. You or I might receive some money or other valuable gift from an estate of a relative who passed away. In this same way, God has written every believer into His estate. Many present blessings along with more to enjoy in heaven later, are ours because of this inheritance.

In vv. 11 and 12, Paul addresses Jewish believers (part of the Church) *we also*. Then in v. 13 he refers to the Gentile believers (more of the Church) *you also*. In v. 14 we see them all together as one family, *our inheritance*. The mystery Paul speaks about later is being revealed in these groupings.

Paul's reference to *we* included the first believers in Christ, who probably accepted the good news about Him in the synagogues. The early converted Jews, such as the disciples and Paul, preached Jesus to fellow Jews. Following his reference to the Jews, Paul addresses his readers who are Gentiles. Both Jews and Gentiles are offered the same incredible gift of belief in Jesus.

I see two meanings here concerning this *inheritance*, both true at the same time, and both belong to us. In looking at two translations, both of these meanings reveal a separate truth. Follow this:

The KJV reads, *"In whom also we have obtained an inheritance."* We have an inheritance *in* Christ, which is correct. We mentioned this earlier in this course.

Notice in the Holman translation, HCSB (a quite accurate version) reads *In Him we were also made His inheritance;* here the inheritance is God's and to benefit Him. The emphasis is that, He loves us so much, *we* are *His* inheritance!

Now read again from the AMP Bible. It includes both thoughts: *In Him we also were made [God's] heritage (portion) and we obtained an inheritance.* (Underline added for emphasis)

In Christ we *have* a wonderful inheritance (1 Peter 1:1-4), and in Christ we *are* an inheritance. We will see this again in v. 18. Understand that each of us is valuable to Him. Think of the price God paid to purchase us and make us part of His inheritance! He prizes *each one* of us. This should encourage you to know that He is blessed because He has you! Here is a thought used by many, and quite remarkable: If you had been the only person born on earth and you had initiated sin, God would have found a way to redeem you and then allow you the choice to accept or reject Him. You are not a mistake or created inferior. God made you. Be comfortable in your skin. He loves you.

Read John 17 and note how many times Christ called us *the people whom You have given Me.* This is quite personal.

- The church is *Christ's body* in Ephesians 1:22-23
- His *building* in 2:19-22
- His *bride* in Ephesians 5:22-23

Christ's future inheritance is wrapped up in His Church.

Think on this—We are "fellow-heirs with Christ" (Romans 8:17), which means that He cannot claim His inheritance apart from us! *Fellow* (joint) infers more than one party.

Paul speaks in v. 12 **we who first hoped in Christ,** and again this is referring to these earliest of Jews who had turned to Christ. Paul is in this group—no longer a separate people—now **"in Christ,"** part of the Church. This was as eye-opener to these early Jews. It may be eye-opening yet today.

Next, Paul turns to the Gentiles, who we will see in **benefit #8** (which is for all true Christians). This also verifies the truth that the gospel came *to the Jew first* (Romans 1:16). However, Paul, a Jew, brought the gospel to the Gentiles.

> **Blessing #8** is in v. 13 *In Him you also who have <u>heard</u> the Word of Truth, the glad tidings (Gospel) of your salvation, and have <u>believed</u> in and adhered to and relied on Him, were <u>stamped with the seal</u> of the long-promised Holy Spirit.*
> (Underlines added for emphasis)

Write this one down . . . . #8 *THE HOLY SPIRIT SEALED ME*

Notice the progression here of how the Ephesians and other Gentiles have been brought to Christ. It is summarized in v. 13 by three words. The whole plan of salvation is in this verse. It tells how the *sinner* becomes a *saint*.

They **Heard**

They **Believed**

They were **Sealed (or Stamped)**

Keep in mind what we mentioned earlier in our study, the Trinity of God is at work in the blessings. The Father *chose us* and *adopted us*, (blessings 2 and 3); The Son *redeemed us, forgave us, revealed God's will to us*, and *made us God's inheritance.* (Blessings 4, 5, 6 and 7).

Now, we complete the nine benefits, with the Holy Sprit's part in our blessings. We already saw His opening overview of all the blessings (Blessing 1). You have all the Spirit's promises—now His part is specific in blessings 8 and 9.

In referring to the Gentiles, first they **heard the Word of Truth.** The Ephesians heard and realized this spiritual birth was also for them. Faith came to them by hearing the Word.

Having first, **heard**, these Gentiles made a commitment to Christ by an act of faith. Faith is contained in His Word which they heard (Romans 10:16). They **believed** by hearing Truth.

Then, as soon as they believed, they were **sealed** with the Holy Spirit. The wording is quite clear; they were sealed immediately upon salvation. You and I were also sealed at that instant also. Your salvation is real, not imagined, or to be thought of lightly. For Him to have "sealed" you means He approved you.

God revealed to and through Paul, his boundless love, which says The Holy Spirit has set a seal on you.

What is this seal? It is many things. You may have heard perhaps all of these but certainly, they are worth noting again. One of my ministries is to remind the household of faith of their position in Christ. Isaiah said **put me in remembrance** (43:26), Peter said **so I intend always to remind you about these things** (2 Peter 1:12), and Jude said in Jude 5 **Now I want to remind you.** Therefore, I remind you—Because you have been sealed, you should have a thorough understanding of it.

Of course, we know that in earlier days, the kings had their own seal. For sure then, our King of the Domain (God has His Kingdom we live and function in), has a Seal.

Some kings had a ring to apply authority to a document. He would press his personal seal into the wax placed on the document. If you had that document, you had all the rights contained in it, because of the king's seal.

I have noted five very specific things the seal represents. I am sure there are more. Note them in respect to what the Holy Spirit did when you accepted Christ:

His seal speaks #1, of **a finished transaction.**

Even in our day, we know most important documents need to be stamped with a seal to signify completion. A Notary performs this action for those documents. Nothing else will seal you any more than your acceptance of Christ. It is a finished transaction. Jesus *notarized* you.

#2, His seal also speaks of **ownership.**

God has put His seal on us because He has purchased us to be His own. God is the **King** of a **Dom**ain, His Kingdom. He owns you and me. So much more could be said about this Domain with its ruler, citizens, and benefits. It is a great study. Dr. Myles Munroe wrote a series of books on this subject.[10]

A King has authority over his subjects and laws.

#3 His seal means **protection and security**

The Roman seal was placed on the tomb following Christ's death, probably on both sides of the tomb. Once it was sealed, no one was to break the seal. Legally that seal protected the tomb 24 hours a day.

Therefore, the believer belongs to God, and is safe and protected because he is part of a finished transaction, a death. Acknowledge that! Claim hold of it. Take it as yours. Moreover, let no one or no thing pull it down with troubles and doubts. (Protection is one our five benefits in Psalm 103).

According to John 14:16-17, the Holy Spirit abides with the believer forever, to **be with you forever.** It is possible for us to grieve the Spirit and lose the blessings of His ministry (Ephesians 4:30), however He does not leave us.

#4 His seal was a mark of **authenticity.**

A signature on a letter confirms it is genuine; so the presence of the Holy Spirit is the confirmation of a believer. You really *are* **in Christ.** You are authentic. Think of who you are: 1 John 3:1 *SEE WHAT [an incredible] quality of love the Father has given (shown, bestowed on) us, that we should [be permitted to] be named and called and counted the children of God!*

John 1:12 *But to as many as did receive and welcome Him, He gave the authority (power, privilege, right) to become the children of God.*

2 Corinthians 6:18 *And I will be a father to you, and you shall be My sons and daughters says the Lord Almighty.*

Romans 8:9 is so important concerning this *But if anyone does not possess the [Holy] Spirit of Christ, he is none of His [he does not belong to Christ, is not truly a child of God].* Also, read Romans 8:14.

#5 meaning to this word seal, **it assures destination.**

God sealed you when you accepted His Son.

When you were born *into* Christ, it was as though the Holy Spirit pressed you into the wax of the blood of Christ and sealed you forever.

This once-for-all act gives us continual assurance that we are God's children and entitled to His riches and goodness. You are with Him *now*, and you are assured of being in His very presence *later*.

Tell the devil who owns you: "Look at the seal on my spirit, I'm owned by the Father God! Don't mess with me!"

You can boldly declare it forth: "I'm owned by the Father, I'm guaranteed in Christ, I have an assured destination! I have all His blessings"!

So, this part of the blessings declares you're *finished and complete, owned by God, protected and secured, absolutely authenticated in Christ, and assured of arriving in His presence!* If that doesn't raise your temperature and stand you on your feet, check your pulse.

> And **Blessing #9** is in ¹⁴ *That [Spirit] is the guarantee of our inheritance [the first fruits, the pledge and foretaste, the down payment of our heritage], in anticipation of its full redemption and our acquiring [complete] possession of it-to the praise of His glory.*

Interesting wording in the Greek *That [Spirit] is the guarantee of our inheritance.* Some versions use "deposit." These are the same words as the giving of an engagement ring. In fact, in Greece today it is still used exactly that way.

The Holy Spirit is the down payment and guarantee of the coming marriage of Christ and His Church.

Write it down: #9 **THE *HOLY SPIRIT HAS GIVEN US AN ENGAGEMENT RING.***

We use the same word (***guarantee***) today as *earnest money*. Think of it as buying a piece of real estate, making a good faith deposit, and placing earnest money through a realtor or bank. My wife and I have done that. I relate that pledge—to what the Holy Spirit did for me. We have an engagement ring from God.

J. Vernon McGraw says it this way: "Earnest money is the money that is put down as a down payment and pledge on a piece of property. It also means that you promise there is more money to follow. The Holy Spirit is our earnest money. He has been given as a pledge and token that there is more to follow in the way of spiritual blessings."¹¹

In a sense, every believer has "God's Property" stamped over the soul. Do not hide it with unbelief or sin. Let it shine forth for all to see. Perhaps it is covered by activities or maybe it is a little faded. I suggest you bring it into full, clear, view.

Of course, no Christian should think, *"Well, I'm sealed, so I can do anything I want."* We must learn to trust the Holy Spirit and listen for His voice. His power is constantly in us so that we can trust God during times of temptation and discouragement. We need to learn and realize that since I am sealed and following the Spirit, I will *only want to do* what is pleasing to Him.

Know that any pledge backed up by the Holy Spirit of God *will occur*. There is coming a day, when it will all be completed, just as God said it would be. God's *earnest money* of the Holy Spirit in our lives is the first payment of all the treasures that belong to us right now, and the assurance of many more.

Then a final summary of Blessing Nine: In v. 14 Paul says **in anticipation of its <u>full redemption.</u>** Our redemption is experienced in three stages.

1. The Scriptures tell us *we were redeemed* and that was our faith in Jesus Christ.
2. We also *are being redeemed* as the Holy Spirit works *in* us to make us more like Christ.
3. In addition, as in v. 14, *we shall be redeemed* when Christ returns and we become like Him. This is our ***full redemption.***

The final words of this long sentence are ***to the praise of His glory.*** What a great way to end this sentence. He started the sentence (v. 3) with ***May blessing (praise, laudation, and eulogy) be to the God and Father of our Lord Jesus Christ (the Messiah).*** Then following his list of our many blessings, Paul returns to where he intended to go. He had been "caught up" in Christ, going back to the beginning of salvation, before the creation of the world. Paul then showed how God chose us in Christ by providing redemption, and how the Holy Spirit applied that work to the individual.

A convenient way to remember your blessings:

From Ephesians Chapter One, I Know, *In Christ,* I AM:	
Blessed	*³ every spiritual blessing*
Chosen	*⁴ He chose us*
Adopted	*⁵ to be adopted . . . . through Jesus Christ*
Redeemed	*⁷ᵃ we have redemption*
Forgiven	*⁷ᵇ the remission (forgiveness) of our offenses*
Enlightened	*⁹ Making known to us*
An Inheritance	*¹¹ were made [God's] heritage*
Sealed	*¹³ stamped with the seal*
Assured	*¹⁴ the guarantee of our inheritance*

ASK: *"Why did God choose you for His blessings?"*

Section One
Additional Questions and Thoughts for Discussion

1. Discuss why Paul wrote the book of Ephesians.
2. Is there any significance in Paul's 'long' sentences?
3. How many of the nine blessings can you name?
4. The blessings in Ephesians 1 are spiritual. How do *spiritual* blessings translate into *everyday* life? What effect should they have on your emotions, relationships, and vocation?
5. Discuss how each Person of the Trinity is involved in your nine blessings.
6. How do you receive these blessings?
7. Does your life reflect a life *in Christ?*

Six

Enlightenment

The first section of our study that we have completed (see Outline in cp. ONE) was **The Believer's Riches in Christ.** This second section of Ephesians is entitled **The Believer's Enlightenment.** It considers the paragraph of Ephesians 1:15-1:23.

We are still detailing our *position*, our place as believers. This is who we are. So far in our study, we have been informed about what our blessings are, but Paul's intent is much more. His intention is to explain that the knowledge *of* them is not enough. Christianity is knowledge, yes, but it is also power.

Beliefs are quite easily attacked. Information, as valuable as it is, or the knowing *about* blessings, is not the final goal. We discovered earlier in our study, that we were "born rich" when we trusted Christ.

I received a Facebook note from a well-known minister just at the time I was writing this chapter. In summary it said "Too many of us know about our inheritance, but few of us live really knowing what it is."

Again, Paul is teaching, "knowledge about" is not enough, for we must grow in the understanding of our riches if we are ever going to use them to the glory of God. We have to read our spiritual bankbook to find out the spiritual wealth that God has put in our account. We have to be taught and then dig deeper.

We grow in understanding. A similar statement by another (unknown) scholar explains it in a similar way: "We have to look into our bank account and read the value of it." Similarly, we as born-again believers, spiritually rich children of God, fail to use the wealth because of a lack of understanding.

Most of you have heard of William Randolph Hearst the newspaper publisher. He owned the San Francisco Examiner and New York Journal. He controlled the largest newspaper business in the entire world.

He invested a fortune in art treasures from around the world. One day he read about a few of the most valuable art pieces ever produced. Therefore, he sent his agent abroad to find them. After spending months and incurring millions in expenses, the agent came to Hearst and said, "I found them all. I found them in your warehouse!" <u>All this expense, all this searching, all this time and Hearst already owned the treasures.</u>

It is indeed one thing to know about the blessings and own them, another thing to walk in to the warehouse, discover what is there, and use what is yours. *Discover the treasure deposited in your heart.*

Paul gave us four prison prayers, one here and another we will read in cp. 3. The other two are Philippians 1:9-11 and Colossians 1:9-12. (We could consider the final few words of Ephesians 6 as a fifth prayer.)

In none of his four prayers (each while under arrest) did Paul request material things. I find that so interesting! His emphasis was on real Christian character, not just knowledge. He never asked God to give believers what they did not have, but rather Paul prayed that God would reveal to them what they already had. Paul knew of their faith and love, and he rejoiced in this. However, he knew that faith and love were only the beginning. The Ephesians needed to know much more. This is why he prayed for them, and for us.

Prayer is simply talking to God. It's a conversation with the almighty God of the Universe, believing that He hears, and that He wants to speak to us. It is easy to talk to Him, but harder to hear, yet He tells us, ***"Call to Me, and I will answer you, and show you great and mighty things, which you do not know"*** (Jeremiah 33:3 NKJV).

Paul wrote his prayer for all believers. He could have said, "I pray for you," and left it at that. Instead, he detailed the different requests he prayed. Through these prayers, they could realize how God was working out those very things in their lives and become encouraged.

I suggest you keep in mind that the Holy Spirit gave Paul's prayer to every believer, to pray for one's self and pray for others. Insert a loved one's name in those prayers.

Before we look at Paul's four requests in this Ephesians 1 prayer, here are *two observations* to keep in mind:

First, "enlightenment" (or revelation, awakening, like a "light bulb turned on"); *enlightenment comes from the Holy Spirit.* The Holy Spirit *is* the "Spirit of wisdom and revelation." You can read about this in Isaiah 11:2, John 14:25-26 and 16:11-12. This is not a natural "mind" thing. Man needs the Spirit to enlighten him (1 Corinthians 2:9-16).

Second observation: This enlightenment of blessings that Paul is caught up with *comes to the heart of the believer.* We will come to v. 18, which reads ***By having the eyes of your heart flooded with light***.

We think of the heart as the emotional part of man, but in the Bible, the heart means the inner man (which Peter teaches about in 1 Peter 3:4 and calls the **hidden person of the heart**). The inner man, the heart or center of man, has spiritual faculties that parallel the physical senses.

I recommend a great book called *The Hidden Man* by E.W. Kenyon[12], with revelation on every page. My earliest understanding of Scripture came from his books.

This inner person, our heart "sees." Did you realize that? Also,

- Psalm 119:18 tells us your heart "can see"
- Hebrews 5:11 says the heart "hears"
- Psalm 34:8 and 1 Peter 2:3 the heart "tastes"
- Philippians 4:18 and 2 Corinthians 2:14 the heart "smells"
- Acts 17:27 the heart "touches"

This is what Jesus meant when He said of the people, ***having the power of seeing, they do not see; and having the power of hearing, they do not hear, nor do they grasp and understand*** (Matthew 13:13). The Spirit of God must open the eyes of the heart.

Smith Wigglesworth said, "The life that is in me is a thousand times bigger than I am outside."[13] Oh God! Make me big inside! Let that be your hope and prayer. Determine to be huge inside.

Here in the Ephesians 1 prayer, Paul begins ¹⁵ ***For this reason, because I have heard of your faith in the Lord Jesus and your love toward all the saints (the people of God),*** ¹⁶ ***I do not cease to give thanks for you, making mention of you in my prayers.***

Sort of like saying, "I give thanks for you saints, and pray all the time for you. When I pray I keep praying these things over and over for you." ***I do not cease.*** This carries a strong sense of thankfulness for his hearers. As you pray for others, allow the closeness of them to encircle you. Thank God for their friendship.

PAUL'S PRAYER FOR BELIEVERS

Paul makes four requests for the hearers in his prayer. ¹⁷ *[For I always pray to] the God of our Lord Jesus Christ, the Father of glory, that He may grant you a spirit of wisdom and revelation [of insight into mysteries and secrets] in the [deep and intimate] knowledge of Him,*

Paul's **first** point: *To Know God More Deeply:* ***in the [deep and intimate] knowledge of Him***

Immediately, we see that we are to pray and believe we receive into our hearts, the Spirit of Wisdom and Revelation in God's revealed spiritual knowledge. Wow! Believe it happens. Pray this way. Each of us needs guidance from the Holy Spirit. It is wonderful to realize He is in us to show us our path. He will lead us as we learn to listen.

We are to understand some things that are deep and hidden from the world. This has a starting point. Nothing is to be done in life, without this **first** point of Paul's prayer: a ***[deep and intimate] knowledge of Him.*** First, we have to intimately know God. Paul knew the Ephesians needed to have a deeper understanding of God if they were to continue their life in Christ. They needed to know:

• How much He loved them

- A fuller understanding of His grace
- How He made them His Sons and Daughters
- His willingness to help them every day

False beliefs and teaching exist:

> The *atheist* claims there is no God for us to know.
> The *agnostic* states that if there is a God, we cannot know Him. Kind of like saying, "God is so far away, you can't know him—too far."

Paul has *met* God in the person of Jesus, and he concludes that we cannot really know anything without the knowledge of God Himself. We have to *know* Him!

I want to know Him! I may know my pastor or know my spouse. Very good, but Paul says we have to know God in a similar way. My wife and I really know each other! She knows what I think. She knows my attitude toward life's events. We need to get with Him and learn about Him and really *know* Him.

Paul in an earlier letter, his longest letter, describes in Romans 1:18 the stages of a man's spiritual decline and concludes it is an *unwillingness* to know God. He says a spiritual falling begins with: **Repress and hinder the truth.** Do not stop 'panting' after God, like the Psalmist said in Psalm 42:1 **my soul pants for You, O God.** Ask God to know Him, seek after Him—knock, knock, and then knock again.

The Ephesus believers were rich in faith and love, but Paul longed for them to have a deeper knowledge and enlightenment of God. This refers back to that William Hurst story, or story of the banker I mentioned in chapter TWO.

What the Ephesians *needed*, and believers *need* today, is the same. Not to know more *about* God, but rather *to know God Himself* more deeply. This is the highest knowledge possible. This is Paul's first request for each of us. To cry out at times "I seek you Lord, my inner man pants after you." Paul in an earlier letter, ended his comments to the Corinthians with a desire for them to have fellowship with the Holy Spirit (2 Corinthians 13:14).

When I was a pastor, I will never forget one Sunday morning. It was one of those teaching times that really "nailed" the subject. Following the service, a person came to me and said "Oh Pastor, I loved that message." I asked her what she learned from it. "Oh I don't remember exactly, but it was just good." I went on asking what had helped her and what encouraged her. The same reply kept coming, "I don't remember, I don't know, it was just good."

As far as I am concerned, I had not helped her at all. We need to go beyond the superficial and get to the "knowing." Inspiration is fine, but if information is not realized, then little good is accomplished.

> Paul's **second** request is the first half of verse [18a] ***By having the eyes of your heart flooded with light, so that you can know and understand the hope to which He has called you;*** His second request is *That We Might Understand The Hope to which He called you.*

We see God's light of understanding, His revelation, is for you to be "lit up" with enlightenment so that you can know and understand some things. ***By having the eyes of your heart flooded with light, so that you can know. ASK:*** *Can you think about a time when God just dropped a revelation into your spirit?*

This word ***called*** is important. ***He has called you;*** Paul used it many times in his letters. It is very clear: God calls us by His grace without any thought of anything else. His grace called out to you. You and I are called out of a world system, and into His Kingdom, by His grace.

Paul never tired of testifying that God called him ***through his grace*** (Galatians 1:15); he reminded Timothy that the believer is called ***with a calling in itself holy and leading to holiness*** (2 Timothy 1:9). God, to every believer, has ***called you out of darkness into His marvelous light*** (1 Peter 2:9), and ***has called you to His [own] eternal glory*** (1 Peter 5:10).

Verse [18] ***so that you can know and understand the hope. Hope*** in the Bible does not leave us with only "I hope so." The actual word means *"an expectation of good things."* We need to have a lot of hope in life! The hope that belongs to our calling should be a dynamic force in our lives, encouraging us to be pure and faithful. We'll see in Ephesians 2 vv. 11-12 it's recorded *at one time*, you **had no hope**, but in Jesus Christ, we have **an ever-living hope** (1 Peter 1:3). Paul prayed that every child of God would have that **hope.** Expect the best for your family. Expect good. Expect a good job. Expect a good day. Paul prays that you will wake up, have the light of hope turned on.

We continue looking at Paul's prayer in Ephesians 1. We noted the Holy Spirit wants our inner man flooded with light. Paul's first two requests were that *we are to know God more deeply* and #2 that *we would know the hope He called us to.*

> In his **third** request, Paul wants us *to know and understand what God's inheritance is.* God gained something, when you said "yes" to Him! This is amazing. Paul's third request is to receive the revelation for every child to **Know what God's Rich Inheritance is**. The last part of [18] **and how rich is <u>His</u> glorious inheritance in the saints (His set-apart ones).** (Underline added for emphasis)

We explained this from v. 11, now Paul repeats and prays that we get it down into our spirit. That God should look on us as a part of His great wealth! How amazing is that? He has a great, beautiful, magnificent wealth of creation. We see it every day in the sky, the trees, and in our family. Heaven will certainly be even more magnificent. With all that, God wants you to know that *you* are *His* glorious inheritance! I can't get my thinking around that. I cannot help but believe God looks at His creation (you), not at all as we may think of ourselves (that creation). He sees beyond *now* to how He made you and what He wants for you.

He looked one time at a coward named Gideon and said **The Lord is with you, you mighty man of [fearless] courage** (Judges 6:12-13). Are you kidding? Gideon certainly was not a warrior—yet. Look to Gideon at that moment and we would not see a much of a **warrior.**

God looks at you and says, "You are part of my inheritance, my riches. You're praise to the glory of my grace." When Christ comes for us, we will become like Him. We will no longer sin—and all our human limitations, physical diseases, disabilities and emotional baggage will be gone forever. That is His glorious inheritance He sees! There is nothing wrong with your seeing yourself in that light right now.

This truth informs us, Christ will not enter into His promised glory until the church is there to share it with Him. He also prayed this in John 17:24 ***Father, I desire that they also whom You have entrusted to Me [as Your gift to Me] may be with Me where I am, so that they may see My glory.***

> Then the **fourth** request Paul prays [19] ***And [so that you can know and understand] what is the immeasurable and unlimited and <u>surpassing greatness of His power</u> in and for us who believe, as demonstrated in the working of His mighty strength.*** (Underline added for emphasis)

His fourth request? *That we might Know God's Power.*

Paul's fourth petition for all saints is that they might have a deep understanding and appreciation of the ***power, which*** God engages to bring all this to pass. Paul offers something to challenge our faith: ***the immeasurable and unlimited and surpassing greatness of His power in and for us who believe.***

This power is so tremendous that Paul uses various words to describe it. He amplifies what he is caught up in. We find these words in the Greek.

- He uses *huperballon* which means "to throw beyond the usual boundary"
- He says it's *dunameos* power as in dynamo and dynamite; a special miraculous power
- He adds *megethos* or big
- It's *energeia* working as in energy; an energy in itself
- It's *kratos* or great and mighty
- And it's also *ischuos* meaning forcefulness or strength

Best related by the translation we are using (AMP) ***immeasurable and unlimited and surpassing greatness***

The well-known Theologian F.B. Meyer said, "It is power. It is His power. It is great power; nothing less would suffice. It is exceeding great power, beyond the furthest cast of thought"[14]

These individual Greek words describe this magnificent greatness of His power *towards* us and *in* us. What good is it to have the inheritance that we talked about, if one is too weak to use it?

What if you are so afraid of robbers that you are unable to enjoy what you have? A thief comes to your front door—and you back away in submission. Do not let failure *come*, do not allow fear or discouragement to *enter*, and do not allow sickness to *attack*. Resist the enemy when he comes; be certain he will come! **The thief comes** John 10:10 tells us.

John Rockefeller, the first billionaire lived on crackers and milk because of stomach problems from worrying about his wealth.

We true believers need to know and then exercise this power. This is the power, which God *used* in our redemption, which *He uses* in our preservation, and which *He will yet use* in our glorification.

It is the same power that brought Jesus out from a grave and which we now see in this great explanation of that power in the parenthesis of vv. 20-21. Paul describes the greatest exhibition of divine *power* the world has ever known. He is talking about divine dynamic, eternal energy, available to us!

He seems to be saying in these verses, *"Saints, believers, you must know this power of God."* We need this power because by nature we are too weak to appropriate this wealth. We have to know and trust this power.

As mentioned, one vital reason we need this power is that there are enemies who want to rob us of our inheritance. We will look at this hierarchy the enemy controls, in Ephesians 6. Paul wanted us to know the greatness of God's power so that we would not fail to utilize it when the enemy attempts to steal from us.

When we lived in Texas, one year a storm brought thirteen inches of rain upon our city. I looked out through a window and saw our mailbox covered in water. As the water crept like a *snake* towards our home, I walked out, stood in the one foot of dry pavement between the *snake* and our garage. In the name of Jesus, I commanded the water to stop. It began to retreat and we knew we had walked in our authority and power.

To give you confidence in that power, Paul gives some thoughts about it in a "parenthesis" of vv 20-22.

THE POWER IN EACH BELIEVER

This power [20] *raised Him from the dead.* This power *seated Him at God's right hand in the heavenly [places].*

In addition, in v. 22 this power *put all things under* Jesus' *feet* and made Jesus *Head of the church.* This is the power Paul drives home. Know His power! It is in every believer.

Wow, such a rich "parenthesis"! It really should be in our Bibles in all CAPITAL LETTERS. Lets Read this again in its full context.

> [19] *And [so that you can know and understand] what is the immeasurable and unlimited and surpassing greatness of His power <u>in and for us</u> who believe, as demonstrated in the working of His mighty strength,* [20] *Which He exerted in Christ when He raised Him from the dead and seated Him at His [own] right hand in the heavenly [places],*
> [21] *Far above all rule and authority and power and dominion and every name that is named [above every title that can be conferred], not only in this age and in this world, but also in the age and the world which are to come.* [22] *And He has put all things under His feet and has appointed Him the universal and supreme Head of the church.* (Underlines added for emphasis)

- We've seen huge bombs and other powerful weapons.
- We've seen the power released because of computers.
- We've seen people, great leaders who have demonstrated real strength and power.
- We know even the creation of the universe and deliverance from a Red Sea was power—however, nothing cannot compare to this power of God.

Paul tells us, v. 19 this is the *power in and for us who believe.* A power above ALL power. The greatest power shortage of our day is not in our gas tanks. It is in our personal lives.

The conclusion of this wonderful section two of Ephesians:

²² *and He has put all things under His feet and has appointed Him the universal and supreme Head of <u>the church</u> [a headship exercised throughout the church],*
²³ *<u>Which is His body</u>, the fullness of Him Who fills all in all [for in that body lives the full measure of Him Who makes everything complete, and Who fills everything everywhere with Himself].* (Underlines added for emphasis)

The meaning of the Church is the mystery that was revealed to Paul. That Church, made up of anyone who accepts Christ, has all the fullness of the power of God working in it collectively and individually!

Section Two
Additional Questions and Thoughts for Discussion

1. Name from memory, Paul's four requests in prayer for believers.
2. Do you spend time in your prayer life in praise?
3. Paul was thankful for what characteristics in the Ephesus believers?
4. Discuss the power demonstrated by God.
5. Discuss what enlightenment in the heart means to you.
6. How can you really 'know' God?
7. What is 'hope' and what does it mean to you?

SEVEN

Dead or Alive

Let's edge in to the third Section of Ephesians, **THE BELIEVER'S VICTORY** that continues **THE POSITION OF THE BELIEVER.** We will review this section in two paragraphs.

Paul opens cp. 2 with another one of his contrasts: life with death. Verses 1 through 7 of Ephesians 2 are the second of Paul's long sentences in the Greek. Most versions today break the Greek into shorter sentences to allow for easier reading. Paul is giving every person a choice between life and death. No other choice is remotely possible. Immediately you and I are faced with this choice. I would think that every individual would choose life. Are you kidding! Many have made a choice and are already living *in Christ*.

I think of the words in Deuteronomy. God had listed blessings *or* curses that would come upon His people. Then He said in Deuteronomy 30:15 ***See, I have set before you this day life and good, and death and evil*** and in Deuteronomy 30:19 ***I have set before you life and death, the blessings and the curses.*** As if they needed help to decide, God gives them a hint: ***therefore choose life, that you and your descendants may live.*** Okay, I guess I will choose life!

Paul will describe the difference between spiritual *life* and *death* in this section of Scripture, one of his many contrasts in the letter. The early readers of this letter faced this choice. Every person reading this letter faces, or has faced this choice.

Notice as we continue how the Holy Spirit organizes this area in groups of fours.

First, an illustration I read several years ago. The highest elevation in the United States is Mount Whitney in California, almost 14,500 feet. From the peak, you can see beauty for miles around. Miles below that peak is Death Valley, the lowest spot in the United States, 280 feet below sea level. During the summer, you could stand on the peak of Mount Whitney with a coat on, and a few miles away, stand in 100 degrees! What a contrast! Paul in Ephesians 2 starts in "Death Valley" and sweeps up to the pleasant top of "Life Mountain."

Verse 1 of cp. 2 begins with words that link this chapter strongly to cp. one. He begins *AND YOU.* The chapter break should not obscure the preceding thoughts that we have studied.

In cp. 1, we watched the mighty power of God as it raised Christ from the grave and crowned Him with Glory.

Now in cp. 2 we will see that the *same power* has worked in our lives, raising us from spiritual death, and seating us with Christ in the heavens. *AND YOU* did He raise! [1] *AND YOU [He made alive].*

Then the great contrast. We could say we moved from "death to life." Transforming Grace.

These first verses of cp. 2, describe God's power in salvation, first for the Gentiles, then for the Jews. The picture is a little strange. Paul talks about *Walking Dead* or *Dead Men Walking.* These Gentiles were dead towards God, but alive in the world.

WE WERE SPIRITUALLY LOST

We can relate here with the Gentile—the picture of the horrible spiritual condition of the unsaved person. This is **WHO WE WERE**. Here are four words that describe these Gentiles, along with you and me, before accepting Him and being made new. After each one of these four, I suggest you say, *"That's not me now."* Silly? Not at all—know who you *are* not who you *were.*

> **#1** you were **dead.** And you can say it, *"That's not me now, I am not dead. I have the life of Christ in me."* Paul says they were

spiritually dead in sin. They were lifeless towards God. You might have looked alive, but inside you were cut off from life.

In the Bible, death always means *separation*. That was a horrible place to be in—like a graveyard. The unbeliever is not sick, he is dead. He has no appetite for food or drink. He doesn't have any pain; can't talk and complain. Dead. Every lost person is dead. Think of it. You and I *were* there.

A lost person living under a bridge is dead, without Christ. The head of a corporation is lost without Christ. They are both the same. One is not more dead than the other is. One may be decayed more outwardly than the other, but both are dead in sin.

Sin was the quicksand of our lives. The spiritually dead person does not have any vital contact *with* Christ. Nor is he *in* Him. He is doing nothing to please God.

Verse 1 **(you were dead) by [your] trespasses and sins.** That is what caused the death. Every sinner is pictured here—sad to say, but the truth. This is what Paul is telling them. Moreover, the dead one does not need *resuscitation*, he needs *resurrection*. He or she can only become spiritually alive through the power of Christ's life in resurrection.

Trespasses and sins caused this spiritual death. One's thoughts, words, and deeds have caused a fall. Sin as used in the Bible, usually means "coming short of God." The two words in Greek, trespasses *(paraptoma)* and sins *(ha marita)* are very similar, but with different meanings. Many times, we use these words in the same sentence to describe the same action.

Trespasses in the Greek, *paraptoma*, is a slip or a fall, such as someone falling on a slippery path. He or she is no longer on the right path. This one slipped off the path. This leads to spiritual death. It may be a willing-walk outside the boundaries of God's path. Paul uses this same word many times, some of which are in this letter, 1:7; 2:1 and 2:5, (translated using various words such as *misdeeds, offenses,* and *shortcomings*). Other references would include Romans 4:25 and 5:15-18. Jesus used the word in Matthew 6:14-15 *trespasses* and Mark 11:25 *failings and shortcomings*. We could think of the meaning as slipping away from the truth.

The second word, sins, *hamarita*, is "missing a target" or falling short of a spiritual goal. You perhaps have aimed and missed the target in a dart game. I remember as a young man, pulling the strings on my bow and releasing an arrow or two and *missing* the target. I remember another time while shooting at and then *missing* those "clay pigeons" after yelling, "pull." We all know what missing the target means. This is the word used in the familiar Romans 3:23 **since all have sinned and are falling short.**

Paul used this word *hamarita* seventeen times in his writings. It usually refers to sinning against oneself or another person. It would be beneficial in your study to read Jesus using this word in Luke 17:3-4. A few of Paul's references are in 1 Corinthians 6:18, 8:12, 15:34 and Romans 5:12 (always translated *sin*). Paul uses the noun form of the word, hamaritia, sixty-four times.

We all are or were, guilty of both *paraptoma* and *hamarita*. We may miss God's standards for His children or fall short and slip from His character being duplicated in our lives. I would encourage you to seek Him and His will in your life. Pray daily: *God I ask your help with every step I take, every breath I take, every situation I face and with every person I meet.*

Of course there are many "missing of targets" that are quite evident. Paul was very explicit in his letter to the Galatians. There he addresses and lists some sins directly, those being mistakes of the flesh. He does this to identify specific sins. [19] **Now the doings (practices) of the flesh are clear (obvious): they are immorality, impurity, indecency,** [20] **Idolatry, sorcery, enmity, strife, jealousy, anger (ill temper), selfishness, divisions (dissensions), party spirit (factions, sects with peculiar opinions, heresies),** [21] **Envy, drunkenness, carousing, and the like. I warn you beforehand, just as I did previously, that those who do such things shall not inherit the kingdom of God.** (Galatians 5:19-21)

OKAY . . . here's your chance again to say it: *"That's not me now"*

#2 you were **defiant**

Notice as Paul continues, he uses next the words **you walked [habitually].** This was adequately translated in the AMP Bible because the Greek's compound of words means, "to walk around in one area all the time."

This was the beginning of your spiritual death, against the will of God. (Remember we looked at Paul's earlier prayer and first on his list was—we are "To Know God").

> This second thought is in v. 2 *In which at one time you walked [habitually]. You were following the course and fashion of this world [were under the sway of the tendency of this present age], following the prince of the power of the air. [You were obedient to and under the control of] the [demon] spirit that still constantly works in the sons of disobedience [the careless, the rebellious, and the unbelieving, who go against the purposes of God].* ³*Among these we as well as you once lived and conducted ourselves in the passions of our flesh [our behavior governed by our corrupt and sensual nature].*

The spiritual death that each of us was experiencing was one of conformity to, and agreeing with, this spirit of defiance. Paul is about to tell us three influences or *forces* in the world that affect every one of us. These forces include various strongholds that attempt to mold our lives. Some of these strongholds are selfishness, deception, cheating, revolting, insubordination, immortality, etc.

That is who the Ephesus believers, along with you and me—**WERE!** *And that's not me anymore!* Say it.

We see **three forces** at work, to encourage man in his defiance. They strive for our attention: the world, the Devil, and the flesh. We have already seen the power to overcome each of these, in 1:19, *surpassing greatness of His power in and for us who believe.* It is by that resurrection power of God displayed in Jesus, which is inside each believer.

ASK: *Do you believe the power for our victory is sufficient?* I hope you believe as I do—that His power in us *can* give us overcoming power against all three forces. James tells us specifically to *Resist the devil [stand firm against him], and he will flee from you* (James 4:7).

#1 The World is a world-system, and this force puts pressure on each person to "follow along." ² *In which at one time you walked [habitually]. You were following the course and fashion of this world.* Jesus said, "I am not of this world," and neither are you! (John 8:23; 17:14). The unsaved has his values in the world. The believer does not. He is not of this world; **they are not of the world.**

The Devil is the second force. Our Scripture says it likes this: **[You were obedient to and under the control of] the [demon] spirit that still constantly works in the sons of disobedience.** I remind us that Satan is *not* omnipresent (everywhere at the same time.) This is comforting to know! Also, do not worry about him getting *in* you. He *oppresses* the believer but does not *possess* him. We will see later in our study that Satan has a vast hierarchy—many associates working *in* unbelievers *and* attacking *you* and *me.*

Satan is called by various names in the Scriptures:

- *Accuser*, Revelation 12:10
- *Enemy/devil*, 1 Peter 5:8
- *Angel of the Abyss*, the bottomless pit, Revelation 9:11
- *Apollyon*, Revelation 9:11
- *Beelzebub*, Matthew 12:24
- *Devil*, Ephesians 4:27
- *Serpent*, Genesis 3:4 and Revelation 20:2
- *Evil one*, Matthew 13:19.[15]

His descriptive names reveal a lot!

Satan has many weapons that he uses against us, because he is a murderer and liar. One of his chief tools is "lies." He is a liar and originator of lies. (John 8:44). When a person believes and practices a lie, he becomes a child of defiance. It was the Devil's lie at the beginning of human history that plunged the human race into sin.

Paul also says here, the spiritually dead followed the *example* of the devil . . . **following the prince of the power of the air.** You and I once followed Satan's way. Say it, *"That's not me now."*

The chief ruler of the hierarchy of evil spirits whose realm is in the atmosphere causes the spiritual dead person to fall low.

Then the **third pressure-force** of the system that draws us to disobedience, **The Flesh.** [3] **Among these we as well as you once lived and** *conducted ourselves in the passions of our flesh [our behavior governed by our corrupt and sensual nature].*

We have heard most of negatives concerning this area. Several on the list from Galatians 5:19-21 come from this force. Perhaps this is the strongest of the three. Paul is not referring to the body; the body is not sinful. He is referring to the fallen nature *in* the natural-born body.

This force would like to control the body and mind and drive us to disobey God. The author has written extensively on this subject in *The Battle in The Combat Zone of Our Mind.*[16] This is a spirit that wants children of defiance.

An evangelist used to preach what he called "a dog is a dog." Of course, because a dog has a dog nature, it behaves like a dog. Why does a sinner behave like a sinner? The Bible calls this nature The **Flesh.** Another list by Paul is in the latter verses of Romans cp. 1. We also read in Romans 8:6 *now the mind of the flesh [which is sense and reason without the Holy Spirit] is death.*

We were defiant. Say it, *"That's not me now"*

Then Paul's description of who we *were* continues. He said #1 **You Were Dead,** #2 **You Were Defiant,** and now in v. 3, **You Were Degenerated**

> [3b] *obeying the impulses of the flesh and the thoughts of the mind [our cravings dictated by our senses and our dark imaginings].* (Underlines added for emphasis)

This unsaved person not *only* does evil (by defying God), but now it is worse; we add the word *degenerated.* The lost person lives to please the desires of the flesh and the mind.

He is incapable of doing good. He is incapable of doing anything to be saved. However, always know the Spirit of God can break in to this degenerate person; however, it will take the constant prayers by others to do so. This person is ruled by the defiance we wrote of earlier. Dictated, controlled, and degenerated. This is the condition in which many unsaved live. Only God can break into that. So we trust Him and ask Him to reach and free the one in this state.

You had better say it right here: *"That's not me now"*

Then Paul gives one more, #4. The last words of v. 3 *We were then by nature children of [God's] wrath and heirs of [His] indignation, like the rest of mankind.* (Or we could say "just as all the other unsaved").

Dead . . . . which causes
Defiance . . . . which leads to
Degenerated . . . which means this one is now,
Damned

Let's journey to a major side-trip here.

At times, we say God reaches out to the lost person no matter what that person has done. That is true. God will accept anyone into His Kingdom. God will never stop drawing him; patience, long suffering, not ever wanting a man to perish. Nevertheless, let me suggest to you that there comes a day when God no longer loves a lost one! Wow, I know how heavy this is. Do not misunderstand this.

God loves a human because He sees *in* that person, the image He created. He loves that image. In fact, if we removed the results of sin from him, it would be hard to over-praise him. God's image, that man . . . would be perfect.

However, sin is like a cancer *in* every man, eating all it can get away with. God still reaches out to that sinner!

Extract that sin, and you have the image of God again. That is why Jesus was the image of God because He was a man without sin. Therefore, I say it this way . . . God loves sinners for what He sees in them of His image. He loves them, not because He is being morally lax, but because He stood and said "Let us make man in our image." He cannot love an unholy thing, yet He does love sinners!

So let me go back and repeat my first statement: There comes a day when God no longer loves a lost one.

Let me explain it differently. Jesus taught the Light will not always shine, and that it is possible to repeatedly reject the light and shut it out. He says *When that time comes, how GREAT is that darkness.* Let me mention the two degrees of darkness according to Jesus, (Matthew 6).

First is a darkness that is absolute . . . where there has never been any light. That is the darkness of the heathen; no light has ever shown.

However, there is a second degree of darkness even more intense. *The darkness that follows rejected light.* Until then God has an outreached hand that does not reject. He never wants an individual to be lost in darkness.

Let me use an illustration. The darkness of the night before the sun is seen is one thing. A man might be out late at night, perhaps stumbles and falls. "I fear to even move in the dark. I'd better just stop. I may stumble over a cliff. I have no light to see my way." There is hope for him . . . the sun will rise. That is the darkness of the heathen. There is hope. He may hear and respond to a message of love or grace.

The second darkness, to which Jesus spoke, was *not* the darkness of the man before the sunrise. This was the darkness of the man who had fled from the sun appearing and was hiding in a moral cave, a rejection-cave; refusing to come out where the light could get to him. The sun had risen, he had seen it—and this man fled into a cave, deeper and deeper until there came a point when the light would no longer be seen.

Consider the action of God in Deuteronomy 31. For example [17] ***Then My anger will be kindled against them in that day, and I will forsake them and hide My face from them.*** [18] ***And I will surely hide My face in that day because of all the evil which they have done in turning to other gods.***

On the other hand, we must consider Nineveh. Nineveh, a large and great city, had only days in existence under judgment from God. However, the Word preached, reached into their darkness and caused a flicker of light to reach them [10] ***And God saw their works, that they turned from their evil way; and God revoked His [sentence of] evil that He had said that He would do to them and He did not do it.*** Jonah 3:10

So understand this—God will always welcome one back. There just is this place of darkness, that the one involved has no urging towards God; God's love is available, just withdrawn from action in the life.

I went on a tour through a cave in Ohio. At one point, being so deep in the cave, the guide turned off the lights! It was so dark I could not see my hand next to my eyes! Perhaps you have experienced this. There is place, when too much rejection of His light removes hope for that individual. He is beyond any Truth or light to make any decision towards God. To emphasize again, prayers of individuals *can* reach this darkness and cause the one walking there, to see a glimmer of light.

So even a good amount of knowledge *about* God and not accepting it, turning from it, or not walking in the light once seen is like walking deeper and deeper into a cave where the light can no longer be seen. Now you can understand the words of Jesus when He said **When the light that is in you turns to darkness, how great is that darkness.**

Now we go back to Ephesians 2:3 and notice Paul changed the pronoun. In v. 2 he used **you walked.** Now he uses **Among these we as well** and **we were.** Paul turns to the Jewish person.

John 3:18 records the words of judgment: **he who does not believe has been judged already.**

The unsaved person is condemned. The judge already passed the sentence, but God in His mercy, is staying the execution. We say it right here, *"That's not me now."*

This leads us to v. 4. A *transformation* is introduced. Man cannot save himself, **but God** in His grace steps forth in v. 4.

With the first two words, a change takes place; the great exchange!

- *Who we were* was exchanged for *who we are*
- Life exchanged for death
- The lost is found
- Light dispels darkness.

We began this chapter by saying it would show a great contrast. Paul described who we all *were* at one time, and we said, *"That's not me now."* Not a pretty picture, but a truthful one. Now a transformation takes place; the power that raised Christ from death causes this transformation.

Read again **But God**. You should love those words! They are life-altering words. Maybe the most important words you have ever read. All along, Paul is contrasting and comparing in these verses of cp. 2 between what happened to Jesus (mentioned in cp. 1) and what happens to Christians. The immense power God revealed in raising Jesus, He has used to do potent spiritual things in believers.

- I was lost—but God!
- I was a sinner—but God!
- I was in darkness—but God!

- I fail Him at times—but God!
- Dead, defiant, degenerated, damned! ***But God.***

But God. In those two words is contained the entire Gospel.

WE ARE ALIVE

We saw who we *were* in the first three verses of cp. 2. Now Paul turns to **WHO WE ARE.**

I would rather concentrate on who I am, study about who I am, and know who I am! I no longer care who I *was.*

I could **ASK:** *Who are you now?* You have to know the depth of this.

Paul in Colossians 3:7 again tells us a transformation is needed; a turning from death to life. ***Among whom you also once walked, when you were living in*** and ***addicted to*** **[such practices]** [8] ***But now put away and rid yourselves [completely] of all these things***: then you can read his list of the "things" in the latter part of v. 8.

If you would ask me, "Who *are* you?" I might answer Tom Hiegel.

> No that's your name.
> "Oh I'm a teacher."
> No, that's what you do
> "I'm a football fan"
> No, that's what you enjoy
> "I'm an American"
> No that's where you live
> "I'm evangelical"
> No, that's your belief system.

I could also say I am 5'9" and 190 lbs. However, my physical height and appearance are not who I am. If you cut out my heart or my kidneys, or my liver, would I still be me? Of course.

ASK: *"Is who you are determined by what you do or is what you do determined by who you are?"*

Paul wants us to realize a transformation took place, from the past to the reality of *now*—from death, defiance, degeneration, and being dammed—into God's Kingdom of love. The focus now is on God—not on humankind before knowing Christ.

We see the *author* of this transformation when he writes **But God.**

No one else could have done it! **But God**
No one else would have done it! **But God**

Who is this God?

God is *sovereign.* He made, and is in control, of everything. Since He is sovereign ruler, nothing happens without His permission. He is not surprised by anything.

God is *holy.* He does not ignore right or wrong. Moreover, because He is holy, everything will be judged. Know that sin will be judged . . . . and righteousness will be exalted.

Then we see here the great characteristic of God that caused it: [4] *so rich is He in His mercy.*

Similar to Paul giving us four statements as to the status of sinners (dead, defiant, degenerated, and damned), he now shares four activities of God in order to save them. This is God's work *for* us. We said, *"That's not me"* after those statements of our past life; now after each of these, I want you to say it boldly *"I'm glad for that."*

1. [4] *Because of and in order to satisfy the great and wonderful and intense love with which He loved us,* his first activity to save a lost person is quite simply **He Loved Me.**

Any gift has the characteristic of the greatness of its giver. A person of integrity gives a worthy gift. A gift of junk—(You fill it in!)

The excellence of God's character towards us is interesting. He *is* love and gives forth that love into each of His children. He gave love to us on a cross. His free grace gives us what we do not deserve. What do you say? "I'm glad for that."

2. He **Made Me Alive.** We were dead and dead men do not rise, *but God* made me alive with Christ.

> [5] *Even when we were dead (slain) by [our own] shortcomings and trespasses, He made us alive together in fellowship and in union with Christ; [He gave us the very life of Christ Himself, the same new life with which He quickened Him, for] it is by grace that you are saved. And He raised us up together with Him and made us sit down together [giving us joint seating with Him] in the heavenly sphere [by virtue of our being] in Christ Jesus.*

This spiritual transformation was accomplished by the power of the Holy Spirit, acting upon the Word, giving us life. We were dead and dead men do not rise—*but God.*

The Scriptures record that Jesus raised three people from the dead. Each time, the Living Word spoke and gave life. The widow's son in Luke 7:11-17, Jairus's daughter in Luke 8:49-56, and Lazarus in John 11:41-46. There is nothing more important than speaking the Word *into* the problem. It always produces life.

Hebrews 4:12 says: *For the word of God is living and active and sharper than any two-edged sword, and piercing as far as the division of soul and spirit, of both joints and marrow, and able to judge the thoughts and intentions of the heart.* Also notice v. 13 *And there is no creature hidden from His sight,*

No one alive can escape the penetration of His living Word. Do not ever give up. Make sure the living Word is read over your situation; somehow, it *will* penetrate (even that cave of total darkness I mentioned).

Ephesians tells us in v5 we are *made alive together . . . with Christ*

When He was made alive, so were we.

When He was raised, so were we.

When He was seated with the Father, so were we!

So, say it right here *"I'm glad for that."* God Loved Me, He Made Me Alive.

3. This next activity towards us is **He Exalted Me.** [6] *He raised us up together with Him made us sit down together [giving us joint seating with Him] in the heavenly sphere [by virtue of our being] in Christ Jesus.*

We are not raised from the dead and left to walk in death. Since we are now *in Christ* and united *to* Him, we are right now exalted *with* Him. Our physical position may be on earth, but our spiritual position is *in the heavenly sphere in Christ Jesus.* We have been called to sit with Him and enjoy His presence! We are exalted! We have been called from death to sit in glory, with Christ *in the heavenly sphere.*

He tells us where *we are,* *made us sit down together in the heavenly sphere.* When He was seated with the Father, so were we!

*   Transforming grace did this!
*   No longer spiritually earthbound!
*   No longer forced to be occupied with the world.

The same power of God, that gave Him resurrection life, has also exalted us.

If you truly understand these two words *but God,* and recall them daily, living by them, you will experience transforming grace.

Look with me at Paul's "new words." I mentioned this earlier in our course. Paul at various times would coin new words. There are three of them in Ephesians 2:5-6. Paul has discussed the radical change in our lives that took place by the grace of God. We *were dead in sins,* but now *made alive with Christ.* Dead, now alive. We were objects of wrath, now recipients of love. What can describe *that?* Therefore, it is not surprising that in Paul's day, adequate words did not exist to express spiritual revelation.

Therefore, Paul originated a few new words. Boyce explains this more thoroughly than I can.[17] Allow me to summarize—Paul took a Greek prefix "sun" (or *syn)* meaning "together with" and combined it with three words he earlier used to describe what Jesus did after the crucifixion.

They are here in our text.

> The **first** word is *sunzoopoieso* (pronounced *so zo paEL)* which means, "to make alive together with"; each of these three words were experienced at our new birth and each is completed with *Him.*
> The **second** is *sunegeiren* (pronounced *SEN A GaLO')* meaning "to raise up together with";
> A **third** word is *sunekatjosen (SOON KA Pezo')* which means, "To sit down together with."

Taken together these words make one of the most magnificent statements in the Bible about what happened to you and me concerning Jesus' work of salvation.

Paul is just overwhelmed here (catch this); he interrupts his train of thought again to exclaim in verse [8] *it is by grace that you are saved!* He already said that in v. 5. Grace saved you. What do you say? *"I'm glad for that"*

4. **He Frees Me**

> [7] *He did this that He might clearly demonstrate through the ages to come the immeasurable (limitless, surpassing) riches of His free grace (His unmerited favor) in [His] kindness and goodness of heart toward us in Christ Jesus.* [8] *For it is by free grace that you are saved (delivered from judgment and made partakers of Christ's salvation) through [your] faith. And this [salvation] is not of yourselves [of your own doing, it came not through your own striving], but it is the gift of God;* [9] *Not because of works, lest any man should boast. [It is not the result of what anyone can possibly do, so no one can pride himself in it or take glory to himself.]*

God frees you! God's purpose in our redemption is *not* to keep us *from* hell, as great a work as that is. That's a great thing, but not *the* thing. He frees us from it. Verses 8 and 9 are one of those "stand alone" passages, containing the greatest message anyone can hear. Its three parts are both vital and simple: *For it is by free grace,* it is *through [your] faith* and a contrast *not because of works.*

His ultimate purpose in our salvation is that for all eternity His Church would glorify His Grace. We are to bring glory to God in all we do. It takes spiritual freedom to do that. We saw that purpose in three Scriptures we read in cp. 1.

1:6 *[So that we might be] to the praise and the commendation of His glorious grace*

1:12 *So that we who first hoped in Christ [. . . have been destined and appointed to] live for the praise of His glory!*

1:14 *That [Spirit] is the guarantee of our inheritance . . . to the praise of His glory.* This is His purpose in redemption.

The phrase *you are saved* in v. 8 is in the *perfect tense*, which expresses a "present permanent state as a result of a past action." In other words, because a Christian makes a one time and firm decision to receive Christ and be forgiven of all sins, he is permanently secure in eternity as a child of God. He is no longer condemned for his sins. That is grace—a gift of God's love. In vv. 8 and 9, Paul will again talk about being saved by grace.

Therefore, as we have seen, God's actions toward each of us are: "He Loved Me", "He Made Me Alive", "He Exalted Me" and "He Frees Me." Let's be glad for each of these!

Then look again at verse [8] *For it is by free grace that you are saved.* Salvation cannot be of works. He says here [9] *Not because of works.* The work of salvation has already been completed on the cross. The work was done by Christ, for us. Sin worked *against* us demanding death, while God worked *for* us creating new life.

We can *know* our salvation; he tells us in [8] *you are saved (delivered from judgment and made partakers of Christ's salvation).* Paul declares it: *you are saved.*

Rick Warren said "The moment you were spiritually born into God's family, you were given some astounding birthday gifts: the family name, the family likeness, family privileges, family intimate access, and the family inheritance!"[18]

Years ago when anyone came forth for salvation, I would have the person say, "I am saved, no longer lost." Say it with your own mouth. Hear those words of profession. Know what it means.

The thought of any person *earning* or working for God's grace to be saved, is rejected by Paul's words of verse [8] ***And this [salvation] is not of yourselves [of your own doing, it came not through your own striving].*** He goes on in that verse ***but it is the gift of God.***

Then read verse [9] ***Not because of works.*** This is a deep and misunderstood area. Back to this topic of works, I offer a list of deeds that some think will be enough! In fact, many *work* toward these things with the hope of being saved! Perhaps at one time, even you believed one or more of these would assure you of a heavenly home:

- Water Baptism
- Church Membership
- Church attendance
- Communion
- Giving to charities
- Being a good neighbor
- Living a moral, respectable life.

You can add to this list I am sure. *Not one* of these in itself assures a home in heaven.

Works or faith and works do not save a person! You are only saved by faith. How profound!

What is this faith that must be used? I find it has three elements that I call **The Head**, **The Heart** and **The Feet** of faith. Briefly, I will elaborate. One **first** receives the good news by hearing the gospel. It *may* include knowledge about the various blessings mentioned by Paul earlier. This is the first element because we can only believe in something by receiving information about it. *The Head.* In the **second** element, our heart responds to the information received. I like to think that what is received in the head then must drop into the heart when it takes root. If it remains in the head, faith cannot be produced. *The Heart.* The **third** element is a dedicated discipline to walk with Christ. This is casting your life upon Christ, walking with Him each day and accepting He is the author, power, and completer of our life. *The Feet*

In Paul's day, there were other possible answers to the question "What is this faith?" As we see in this paragraph in Ephesians, one answer was "by good works." Paul would have answered that way before meeting with Christ. He changed his answer! He found out all his good works could not cancel out bad things. He could not earn God's grace by following every one of God's laws. (You can read his thoughts in Romans 3:27-31).

> Let's read v. 10, which completes this paragraph started in v. 1. *For we are God's [own] handiwork (His workmanship), recreated in Christ Jesus, [born anew] that we may do those good works which God predestined (planned beforehand) for us [taking paths which He prepared ahead of time], that we should walk in them [living the good life which He prearranged and made ready for us to live].*

Paul has talked about many blessings in his letter. Now he wants to make sure his audience understands. Not one of those blessings is earned. It's a matter of applying Jesus' death to you and then trusting that God has done all the rest. He does the saving and securing. He does the "gracing" that raises one from death to life and showers with benefits. This has nothing to do with being good enough to deserve or earn a place in heaven, because no one can be that good.

However, we *do* good works as an outward exclamation of His work in our lives. We are saved, becoming like Him to show His life that is in us.

These verses continue with the subject **WHO WE ARE** and show God's work *in* us. *For we are God's [own] handiwork (His workmanship)*

This of course is the result of vv. 7, 8 and 9, a new life of salvation.

This handiwork is God's doings! Not ours. A born-again person is a masterpiece! The Greek word we have here, as *handiwork* is really the English word "poem." What a wonderful thing to know about ourselves. God continues to work in us to make us what He wants us to be—like Christ! We are His ongoing, always improving "poem."

There was a great composer George Handel. He was handed several verses of Scripture and asked, "Can you make entertainment out of it?"

Handel took the words, rearranged the verses, and wrote music so fast the ink was not dry before going on. As Handel finished the work he called "The Messiah" he said, "I do not remember whether I was in my body or out of my body when I wrote it." Handel's great Messiah, has been considered a great masterpiece for the last 250 years.

[10] *For we are God's [own] handiwork (His workmanship)*

You are not ugly!

You are not useless!

You are not hopeless!

You are not worthless!

Kay Arthur has written, "You are not an accident! You are not useless. You are not worthless. You are not unredeemable. Your worth and purpose in this life do not depend on who you are, on what you have done, or on what has been done to you. Your worth and purpose do not depend on where you have been, even if you have been to the very precipice of hell."[19]

I would **ASK:** *What does Christ want of you?* Ponder it the next few minutes.

Each of us is an inspired creation of God. God's masterpieces will last forever. His masterpieces intend for His artistry to always be seen and heard.

Think back at the raw material He had to work with, and it becomes all the more remarkable.

ASK: *Are you at peace, with who you are?*

2 Corinthians 5:17 is that wonderful verse: *Therefore if any person is [ingrafted] in Christ he is a new creation (a new creature altogether); the old has passed away. Behold, the fresh and new has come!*

Then continuing in Ephesians 2:10, even though good works did not create us, we are His workmanship; we *were* created *that we may do those good works*.

Before our conversion, God mapped out a plan for each one of us. *Our* responsibility is to find His will and then do it. Examine your gifts and abilities that God birthed into your new life. Use them to walk in the plan God has for you. If you make wrong decisions or plans, take it to God and tell Him you may have "blown" it, and move on with His guidance.

Another question to **ASK:** *Is there only one path for your life?*

Some may balk at that. "It's too hard to discover." "I don't really believe His plans for me can be located!" "Too difficult".

May I suggest a method of how you and I can know what the works you are to do? We all should have done this. If not, do it before you go further in this study.

> **First,** confess any sin that you are conscious of in your life
> **Continually** be yielded and open to Him
> **Study the Word**, read it, and listen for His direction
> **Pray** every day
> Then **do** what you are impressed to do *without hesitation*

Also, notice in v. 10, two characteristics of our works—first they are ***good*** in contrast to what we earlier saw in v. 1 where our works were ***dead (slain) by [our own] shortcomings and trespasses.*** Now the works are ***good*** because the saved one is good himself.

Then not only are they ***good***, they are also ***prearranged*** or prepared for us. The only other time this word is used in the New Testament is Romans 9:23 which says ***He thus purposes to make known and show the wealth of His glory in [dealing with] the vessels (objects) of His mercy which He has prepared beforehand for glory.*** We are to walk in the good works and ways that God has prepared. We have to act on what Scripture declares and what the Holy Spirit prompts.

The first ten verses in cp. 2, traced the salvation of Jews and Gentiles, as individual groups. Paul looked at each separate group. All of them were *walking dead* at one time. So Paul says to them 'get out', 'get alive', 'get new', 'get changed', 'GET IN CHRIST'.

EIGHT

Peace Mission

The second paragraph in the third section (The Believer's Victory) of study is vv. 11-22 of cp. 2. Paul's thoughts are concerning this union of all believers who are in Christ. Paul continues into the uniting of Jews and Gentiles to form a holy temple in the Lord. We moved out of spiritual death, to a new life, and now to peace in that life.

> ¹¹ *Therefore, remember that at one time you were Gentiles (heathens) in the flesh, called Uncircumcision by those who called themselves Circumcision, [a mere mark] in the flesh made by human hands.* ¹² *[Remember] that you were at that time separated (living apart) from Christ, utterly estranged and outlawed from the rights of Israel as a nation, and strangers with no share in the sacred compacts of the [Messianic] promise [with no knowledge of or right in God's agreements, His covenants]. And you had no hope (no promise); you were in the world without God.*

The first 10 verses taught on salvation and how it is available to everyone. Now he turns to Christ's work for Gentiles in particular. Most of the Christians in the church at Ephesus were Gentiles.

Now Paul reminds the Gentiles, they were outcasts as far as the Jews were concerned. Some repetition of what we have already seen, so we will move quickly through it. Look at this word picture of the Gentiles:

Separated
Estranged
Outlawed
Strangers
No hope
In the world, without God

The Gentiles were despised. **Gentile:** Any person who is not a Jew. The Jews *called* them the *Uncircumcision*.

They were not physically marked as God's covenant people were marked. *Uncircumcision*, was really a "slur" towards Gentiles.

Look at David's comment in 1 Samuel 17 ²⁶***And David said to the men standing by him, What shall be done for the man who kills this Philistine and takes away the reproach from Israel? For who is this <u>uncircumcised</u> Philistine that he should defy the armies of the living God?*** (Underline added for emphasis)

As mentioned, the Jews in Paul's day called the Gentiles the *Uncircumcision.* It was as though a great valley separated the Jew on a mountaintop from the Gentile *below* in a valley. If a Jew married a Gentile, the Gentile was not acknowledged and was considered dead! A Jew daring to enter a Gentile's home was considered unclean from that moment on. Think about how the Jews thought of Jesus, when He entered homes of non-Jews.

Even so, it was possible for a Gentile to become part of the Jewish religion by being a "proselyte". Those who wanted to worship the Jewish Lord God were allowed to do so. Even *then* they were not granted access to the main Temple. Instead, they were only allowed to worship in the Court of the Gentiles. Therefore, Paul makes it clear to his readers. The Gentiles were ***separated (living apart) from Christ,*** that is, far away from the main center of worship.

The Jews called themselves the *Circumcision*—and Paul objects to this, he takes exception by saying, [***a mere mark] in the flesh made by human hands.*** He wrote in Colossians 2:11 that those who have trusted Christ have received a spiritual ***circumcision not made with hands.***

Paul says it was merely physical, and not a big deal. In the eyes of the Jews, "We are The People," the Gentiles were *not*. Gentiles were thought of as revolting. Paul in v. 11 reminds the Gentiles they were formerly despised.

One word describes this—the word ***without.*** And we will see five additional phrases that will amplify what is being said.

GENTILES

He says you Gentiles were "**without Christ,**" [12a] ***separated (living apart) from Christ.*** They had no Messiah. They were "aliens" from the commonwealth of Israel. Their religion was totally pagan.

The Jews had a Hope. The Scriptures said they hoped in a Messiah. They were in God's plan—the Gentiles were not. The Gentile had no hope of a Savior.

A ***stranger*** (v. 12) to the Jew was one who does not belong, a foreigner having no rights.

In addition, they were "**without citizenship**": [12b] ***no share in the sacred compacts of the promise [with no right in God's agreements, His covenants].*** God had built the Jews into a nation and gave them His law. This was not so with the Gentiles.

We also see here they were a people "**without compacts.**" Covenants were not made between God and Gentile nations. Therefore, the Gentiles were aliens and strangers, and the Jews never let them forget it. The Pharisees would pray every day, "O God, I give thanks that I am a Jew, not a Gentile." Paul was referring to the different covenants that the Lord had made with His people, the Jews, over the centuries. There were four main covenants:

1. *The Noah Covenant* from Genesis 6:22; 7:5, 9, 16; 8:17
2. *The Abrahamic Covenant* Genesis 12:1-3; 13:14-17; 17: 1-10; 55:1-19
3. *The Moses Covenant* Exodus cps. 19-24
4. *he New Covenant:* Jeremiah 31:31-34; Ezekiel 36:24-30[20]

Note in v. 12 ***compacts of the promise.*** Notice it is singular, ***the promise.*** Even though there were several covenants, Paul is quite possibly referring to the promise of The Abrahamic Covenant, since he has been writing mostly about Jews. In that prime Old Testament Covenant, *God said all the families and kindred of the earth be blessed [and by you they will bless themselves].*

In addition, they were "**without hope**"; [12c] *had no hope.* A person without hope! How tragic, but that is exactly what Paul says concerning a person without Chr**ist**. Without hope, one is lost. Without hope, there is nothing.

Finally they were "**without God**"; [12d] *you were in the world without God.*

This is not labeling them atheists. Paul is saying the Gentiles were living without God in a godless world. It was said in that day, it was easier to find *a god*, than a man. Paul wrote in 1 Corinthians 8:5 *For although there may be so-called gods, whether in heaven or on earth, as indeed there are many of them, both of gods and of lords and masters.* In Genesis, Gentiles were intentionally separated by God from Jews, so that it would later be possible for them to be saved. We are told in John 4:22, *Salvation is of the Jews.*

> Then again, those wonderful words of transition in verse [13] *But now in Christ Jesus, you who once were [so] far away, through the blood of Christ have been brought near.*

We saw in cp. 1 v. 4 the transition *But God*; here he similarly uses *But now.* Both have the same emphasis.

Paul describes the greatest peace mission in history: Jesus Christ not only reconciled Jews and Gentiles, but He reconciled both *to* Himself in the one body, the church.

"Reconcile," means "bring together." *Sin is a separator, blood is a reconciler.*

Paul says *now* they are *in Christ Jesus* brought about *through the blood of Christ,* and when that conversion took place, His blood was credited to *their* account.

A NEW SOCIETY

When they were ***brought near*** (v. 13), it was the beginning of a new society. The separation between Jews and Gentiles was forever abolished. You and I can also say, "I am brought near to God." God had put a difference between Jews and Gentiles so His purpose in salvation might be accomplished—once that was done, there was no more difference.

> ¹⁴ ***For He is [Himself] our peace (our bond of unity and harmony). He has made us both [Jew and Gentile] one [body], and has broken down (destroyed, abolished) the hostile dividing wall between us,***

Notice ***He . . . is [Himself] our peace***. It does not say He made peace, while that many times is true.

This says He Himself is our peace. How is it possible, that a *person* can be peace?

Paul explains it: When a Jew becomes a believer—he leaves his nationality behind, he is joined into Christ. When a Gentile becomes a believer, he too leaves any nationality behind, and is grafted into Christ.

The two, once divided by enmity are now ***both [Jew and Gentile] one [body].*** Their union with Christ unites them with one another. Therefore, a Man ***is [Himself] our peace*** just as Micah said in cp. 5 v. 5 ***And this [One] shall be our peace.***

Once divided now unified—by the Man of Peace, the One who *is* peace. Accept the One who is peace, and you become peace with the One.

Then Paul goes on and details the three-fold work of Christ in vv. 14-18:

First-fold work. Jesus made ***both [Jew and Gentile] one [body].*** They should never be called "Jewish Christians" or "Gentile Christians." That would still be a division. They are now Christians, one body, the Church.

Second-fold work. Described in the next words of ¹⁴ ***and has broken down (destroyed, abolished) the hostile dividing wall between us,***

Not a literal wall, of course, but the invisible barrier set up by the Mosaic Laws, which separated Israel from the nations.

The temple actually had 'no trespassing' signs directed to anyone not a Jew. In a sense, there *was* a real wall separating them, a wall of laws. However, Jesus did away with it. Archeologists have discovered the inscription from Herod's temple *"no foreigner may enter within the barricade which surrounds the sanctuary. Anyone who is caught doing so will have himself to blame for his ensuing death."* The Jewish historian Josephus confirms that there were several such inscriptions in the stone walls[21]. Paul once crossed this wall and they threatened to kill *him* (Acts 21:28-31).

Of course, when Jesus died on a cross, the actual veil in the temple was literally torn in two, from top to bottom (Matthew 27:51). No man could have done that. The veil or curtain was six inches thick! Jesus removed the legal barrier that separated Jew from Gentile. I love Romans 10:12-13, [**No one] for there is no distinction between Jew and Greek. The same Lord is Lord over all [of us] and He generously bestows His riches upon all who call upon Him [in faith]. ** [13] **For everyone who calls upon the name of the Lord [invoking Him as Lord] will be saved.** Jesus removed sin. There is no barrier of sin between God and man.

Third-fold work. [15] **By abolishing in His [own crucified] flesh the enmity_[caused by] the Law with its decrees and ordinances [which He annulled];**

Enmity is *deep-rooted hatred.* The Greek word is the opposite word of agape (or God's true love).

Paul says the reason for the hatred was the Law with its decrees and ordinances.

Anti-Semitism was the result—the Law created arrogance as the Jews miss-used their *position* of "God's Chosen People."

The Gentiles hated them for it, while the Jews allowed it to "puff their selves up."

> Then he repeats in [15b] **that He from the two might create in Himself one new man [one new quality of humanity out of the two], so making peace. ** [16] **And [He designed] to reconcile to God both [Jew and Gentile, united] in a single body by means of His cross, thereby killing the mutual enmity and bringing the feud to an end.**

The redemption and reconcilement, was complete; Jew and Gentile, Body of Christ and God, all spiritually infused together as one!

Note how Paul repeated the word *one* to emphasize the unifying work that Christ did.

> *made both one* 2:14
> *one new man* v. 15
> *one body* v. 16
> *one Spirit* v. 18
> Then in v. 19, *one nation* and *one family*.

There is no longer any spiritual division—all was overcome by Christ.

Interesting to note:

> In v. 14 Christ **is** our Peace
> v. 15 Christ **made** Peace
> In addition, v. 17 *He came and preached* peace
> His *first words* after rising from the dead were "*Peace to you*,"
> three times in John 20

Every believer can walk with peace in life to rule over every situation faced. Paul tells the Colossians in 3:15 *And let the peace (soul harmony which comes) from Christ rule (act as umpire continually) in your hearts [deciding and settling with finality all questions that arise in your minds, in that peaceful state] to which as [members of Christ's] one body you were also called [to live]. And be thankful (appreciative), [giving praise to God always].*

The proof that peace exists between the Body of Christ and God is given in verse [18] *For it is through Him that we both now have an introduction (access) by one [Holy] Spirit to the Father [so that we are able to approach Him].* How can we fully describe what God did through Jesus' work on the cross? Before the work, we were strangers, foreigners, and separated from God. In that state, we had no hope. We faced an end in spiritual death. Nevertheless, God *reconciled* and *restored* us with Him through the work on the cross. The veil/curtain was removed—we are free to return to God.

¹⁹ *Therefore you are no longer outsiders (exiles, migrants, and aliens, excluded from the rights of citizens).* Never again will they be strangers, dogs, or the uncircumcision. No longer would they be outsiders, rather they would share citizenship with all saints. We all have a common citizenship.

We are all first class citizens of heaven. Jewish ancestry had no advantage over the Gentile any longer.

¹⁹ *and you belong to God's [own] household.*

We all have a common family, the Church, which is described in Ephesians.

ASK: *What is the Church?* Glance at Paul's view of the Church:

1:11 *for we had been foreordained.* He chose a people who will rule with Him. You become a member by accepting Christ.

1:22 *appointed Him the universal and supreme Head of the church.* Jesus is the universal Head of His Church.

2:21 *In Him the whole structure is joined (bound, welded) together harmoniously.* One body joined in unity regardless of social or cultural differences.

3:19 *that you may be filled [through all your being] unto all the fullness of God.* God's love and all He *is* dwells in His Church.

4:3 *keep the harmony and oneness of [and produced by] the Spirit in the binding power of peace.* We are to live with each other in peace.

4:16 *For because of Him the whole body . . . . grows to full maturity, building itself up in love.* Each member of the body (Church) matures, contributes, and serves each other.

4:24 *And put on the new nature (the regenerate self) created in God's image, [Godlike] in true righteousness and holiness.* We become new creatures and *live* Him before the world.

Paul's theology of the Church included three terms:

1. 1 Corinthians 12:12 *Body*; therefore, it is a living organism and subject to the Head, Jesus Christ.
2. Ephesians 5:23 *Bride* of Christ; therefore it is a loving relationship in which the caring Bridegroom provides for all the needs of the bride.

3. Ephesians 2:21-22 **Building**; therefore it represents a habitation, a temple for the Spirit of God to indwell.

We also notice three images in the book of Ephesians to remind us of who we are in Christ: Body, family, and temple. Each of these images picture believers as *unified* and as being *with* Jesus. The Church as a **body** (3:6), which pictures us working together for the good of each part. The Church as a **family** (2:19) which reminds us we are to live in love, relate to each member, and mature and grow together. The **temple** (2:20-21) shows we are to worship God and bring to Him our praise and service.

Keep in mind, a single, unified church will be with Christ on the eventual "new earth." It will not be a divided body with individual groups. The Lord will be there with those who accepted Him and living for Him. This single Body will have no Muslims, Buddhists, atheists or Christians. It will be the Church.

I like how Paul describes this common family in v. 20: It is being built on **the foundation of the apostles and prophets,** not referring to the Old Testament, but of those of the New Testament.

Paul concludes this thought of "unity" in the final three verses of cp. 2. We saw where Paul repeated the word "one" to make this very clear. In the final three verses, he brings it all together with the term "one temple." This carries such a deep meaning.

> In Genesis 1 God *walked* with His people (Genesis 5:22, 24; 6:9), but from Exodus on, He would *dwell* with them—a tabernacle, a temple, and then the body of Christ. Paul developed this thought around *The Foundation* and *The Cornerstone.* The strength of a building rests on its foundation—that foundation being Jesus (1 Corinthians 3:11). The apostles and prophets were the first witnesses to the Church built upon Jesus. The unity of His Church can only be built on true doctrine. Paul also uses The Cornerstone. The cornerstone fixed the angle of the building. Isaiah 28:16 **Behold, I am laying in Zion for a foundation a Stone, a tested Stone, a precious Cornerstone of sure foundation.** Moreover, Jesus applied the words of the Psalmist in 118:22 to Himself: **The stone which the builders rejected has become the chief cornerstone.**

As you review cp. 2, you cannot help but praise God for what His grace did for you. It raised us from the dead and seated us on His throne in a unified body.

Section Three
Additional Questions and Thoughts for Discussion

1. What does it mean to you to say, "I was dead?"
2. Would you volunteer to describe what your life was like in your period of 'spiritual death'?
3. Discuss Satan's names.
4. The author used four words to describe a person's descent into death. What were they?
5. There are many decent people in the world. How are they influenced by the devil?
6. How does one move from death to life? How is one saved? What Scriptures back your belief?
7. Discuss who you are as a believer.
8. What does it mean to say, "I am seated with Christ in heavenly Places?"
9. What did the Jews think about the Gentiles, and how were they described?
10. Discuss the word 'peace'; its worldly meaning today and its meaning to the believer.
11. How am I bringing peace to those I meet?

NINE

Secret Revealed

The last section of **The Position of The Believer** begins with cp. three of Ephesians, entitled **The Believer's Maturity** (refer to outline in Chapter ONE). As we move into this chapter of Ephesians, notice the interesting structure. We will review this section, in two paragraphs, the first one covering vv. 1-13. The structure begins with another one of Paul's long sentences, most of which is an interruption in his teaching. He is about to pray for them, but a beautiful thought leads him to this "parenthesis" of vv. 2-13. He seems to momentarily be carried away with this important issue. This very important message is that God wants everyone to experience God's grace—the mystery of both Jews and Gentiles alike being a part of one body.

This is the precise detail of the mystery, which is unfolded to Paul. He previously introduced the thought in 1:9-10. Later he will review the mystery in 5:32. The same revelation of the Church is consistent in this letter, however—here in cp. 3 he explains the doctrine. He mentions "mystery" four times in cp. 3 and nineteen more times in his other writings. It is important to understand the important mystery Paul speaks about in cp. 3. This word does not have the same meaning in English and Greek. The English *mystery* means puzzling, obscure or dark. The Greek word *mysterion* is different; it is no longer unknown and hidden. In the New Testament, it is a "sacred secret" that is unknown to unbelievers, but understood and treasured by the people of God.

In this paragraph, Paul explains this mystery—*the Gentile believers are now united to the Jewish believers in one body, the Church.* This was an extraordinary revelation in Paul's life. He explains the reality in two words: He says in v. 1 he's a ***prisoner*** and then in v. 6 he says he's a ***minister***. In a way, this is what each one of us can say. We are captured by Christ, but free to live a full and joyful life, and free to minister.

Paul is praying his second prayer in Ephesians and we look at the unusual structure. He begins a statement, [1] ***for this reason*** that is immediately interrupted in v. 2, and not resumed until v. 14. Therefore, you could place vv. 2-13 inside a parenthesis in order to understand it better. I have done that in my Bible. Verse 14 will again pick up the prayer with the same words ***for this reason.***

It is unfortunate a break occurs between cps. two and three because the thoughts are connected. His words ***for this reason*** are referring back to the great privilege which believing Gentiles are brought into—Christ. They have come *into* Christ, something not even considered before.

> We do learn some new things here; first concerning Paul being a prisoner ***I, Paul, the prisoner of Jesus The Christ***, and second, the reason for the imprisonment for ***the sake and on behalf of you Gentiles***

It is certain Paul was in Roman captivity when he penned this (Acts 28). We know he was in prison more than one time (Philippians 1:13; Colossians 4:18) in his ministry. Paul's final hours were spent in a dark and dingy hole not fit for any man to inhabit. The smell of dried blood and sweat permeated the stones. Indeed, Paul knew about a Roman cell. They were nothing like the prisons of our day. Paul wrote much of his revelation from a dark, dreary cell. However, he was not after pity or sympathy; he had a Comforter with Him, the Holy Spirit. Paul said he was a prisoner of Jesus. This was dignity and triumph not defeat. It was virtually a privilege for Paul to be a prisoner for Christ! He was in a prison because of taking the good news to the Gentiles! A privileged prisoner! Ironic isn't it?

ASK: *How do you describe being a prisoner for Christ?*

I like to think of being a prisoner of Christ. We are not a physical or mental prisoner of difficulties on earth. Not a prisoner of troubles. Not a prisoner of lack. You are a prisoner of no man, only of Christ. If you're a prisoner of Him—you are not behind prison bars or gates. Being *in Christ* is true freedom.

We also understand in this paragraph (v. 2), Paul was given a stewardship of a new dispensation called *grace*. Remember grace is receiving benefits that are underserved. We sometimes connect the word mercy with grace. However, the definition of mercy is: *Not* receiving what we *do* deserve.

God revealed this personally to Paul, and it was his responsibility to share it with Gentile Christians. This was the "dispensation" or stewardship that God had given him. *Because* he was faithful in his assigned ministry—he was led by Roman soldiers to captivity in Rome. Later he will use the description of the familiar Roman clothing to illustrate our spiritual clothing. Led to a prison! Wouldn't you think faithful Paul would have been led to a resort? Maybe the world's greatest missionary would be led to a white sandy beach and palm trees? Perhaps an all night buffet on a ship? Faithfulness does not escape possible imprisonment.

> Now let's read this entire first area in context: The first five verses [1] *FOR THIS reason, I, Paul, [am] the prisoner of Jesus the Christ for the sake and on behalf of you Gentiles* [2] *(Assuming that you have heard of the stewardship of God's grace that was entrusted to me [to dispense to you] for your benefit,* [3] *[And] that the mystery (secret) was made known to me and I was allowed to comprehend it by direct revelation, as I already briefly wrote you.* (Probably referring to Ephesians 1).
>
> [4] *When you read this you can understand my insight into the mystery of Christ.* [5] *[This mystery] was never disclosed to human beings in past generations as it has now been revealed to His holy apostles and prophets by the [Holy] Spirit.* (Note in parenthesis added by author)

Notice how clearly Paul explains the mystery and then details it beginning in v. 3. *This is the most complete definition we have of what Paul calls a mystery.* Paul was entrusted with the message of God's grace:

He says it clearly in ⁶ *[It is this:] that the Gentiles are now to be fellow heirs [with the Jews], members of the same body and joint partakers [sharing] in the same divine promise in Christ through [their acceptance of] (the Gospel).*

It certainly was known in the Old Testament that Gentiles could be saved. However, the concept of Jews and Gentiles joined in one body, the Church, was never disclosed. Paul says it is now being uncovered and made clear. Paul wanted to make sure Gentiles understood the importance of their "membership" in the body of Christ.

We learn more about Paul as he turns to a personal testimony in verse ⁷ *Of this Gospel I was <u>made</u> a minister.*

> He did not make himself a minister
> No man made him a minister
> He did not choose it. It was God's gift!

This word minister is a little misleading here. It's the word usually translated "servant."

That is why we can all relate to this area of Scripture. *A prisoner . . . yes. A servant/minister . . . yes.*

Paul is saying he served the Lord in connection with his assignment, the mystery. He was faithful to deliver what he was given. He was a faithful minister of his gift. Again I refer to the two words we have read that describe Paul, and all believers. Paul was a *prisoner* and a *minister/*servant.

> A good lesson for you and me.

Paul continues ⁸ *I am the very least of all the saints.*

This is a truthful picture of anyone who is filled with the Holy Spirit. When Christ is seen in His glory, we *fade into Christ.* The Holy Spirit gives us an awareness of Jesus that sets *self* aside. We see ourselves when we pray. Some self-examination takes place. Paul says *I am the very least.*

Probably because he had intentionally persecuted Christians—Paul now he realizes what he had done.

He wrote to Timothy in 1 Timothy 1:13 and said *"I was formerly a blasphemer and a persecutor and a violent aggressor . . . ."* the very least.

He also said *"But by the grace of God I am what I am . . . ."* (1 Corinthians 5:10) the **least** because he is **in Christ.**

The word **unending** in verse ⁸ **unending riches of Christ**, offers us a beautiful picture. In the Greek, the word, *anexichníaston* conveys the idea of "leaving no footprints". If someone was able to walk alongside the seashore and not make any footprints in the sand, he could not be searched for and found. In like manner, the full benefits of knowing Christ can never be completely searched for and found. In addition, even if some benefits are discovered, there are many more. Other translations have used "unsearchable", "unending", "unfathomable", and "endless". It is hard to describe or even imagine the riches we have as a result of being **in Christ.** *What eye has not seen and ear has not heard and has not entered into the heart of man, [all that] God has prepared (made and keeps ready) for those who love Him.* (1 Corinthians 2:9).

> Verse 10 is a powerful verse that this new unified Body of Christ is to know and act upon. *The purpose is that through the church the complicated, many-sided wisdom of God in all its infinite variety and innumerable aspects might now be made known to the angelic rulers and authorities, principalities and powers in the heavenly sphere.*

One of God's purposes in relation to this mystery goes beyond telling the whole world about this unity in Christ; it is also to reveal the many sides of His wisdom *to* angels, both the good ones and the bad ones! There are many things angels do not know!

We have a picture here of angels viewing, perhaps for the first time, the Church and God's plan for it. They now see how God has triumphed over sin. They see that He sent Heaven's best for earth's worst! Angels did not know the extent of God's plan!

He redeemed you and me at an enormous cost, conquered a people by love, and prepared them as a Bride for His Son.

He has blessed us with all Spirit-given blessings. The many blessings to Jews and Gentiles are now revealed to angels. This is greater than if sin had never been even allowed to enter humanity. Now a willing human being accepts and becomes something new. This is greater.

Angels now see Christ exalted, Satan defeated and the Church enthroned in Christ and share His Glory.

What a picture, *now revealed* to angels!

One commentator says, *"The history of the Christian Church is a graduate school for angels."*[22]

We will consider much more about Satan and his angels in Ephesians cp. 6, but it is mentioned here in v. 10: The Body is to tell those *dark* angels also! We have been redeemed and are blessed of God and we tell the fallen angels what He has done!

Keep in mind v. 12 as we close this paragraph in Ephesians:

> *In Whom, because of our faith in Him, we dare to have the boldness (courage and confidence) of free access (an unreserved approach to God with freedom and without fear).*

Here we see every believer, at any time, has the privilege of entering into God's presence with boldness. *"Come before His presence"* (Psalm 100:2) the Bible says. We saw in 2:6 of Ephesians that we are seated *with* Christ.

> Verse 13 concludes *So I ask you not to lose heart [not to faint or become despondent through fear] at what I am suffering in your behalf. [Rather glory in it] for it is an honor to you.)*

You *never* need to give up, *never* need to give in, to fear. Paul says I am suffering some right now, but it is an honor, so do not fear! The Scriptures are full of assurances of a fear-free life. (Judges 4:18; 2 Kings 6:16; Psalm 23:4, 46:2).

I'm reminded of that wonderful phrase in Isaiah 43:1 *. . . thus says the Lord, He Who created you, . . . and He Who formed you, . . . : Fear not, for I have redeemed you I have called you by your name; you are Mine.*

TEN

Take Your Wealth

The second paragraph, which completes cp. 3 of Ephesians, is Paul's concluding remarks concerning **The Position of the Believer**. By now, you have realized a few revealed facts that Paul repeats, however each is presented with a different viewpoint. I mentioned an area earlier in our course: You and I must do more than only understand our wealth—we have to "take hold of it."

Paul's second prayer in Ephesians deals with *enablement* while the first prayer we reviewed in cp. 2 vv. 15-23 dealt with *enlightenment*. It is not so much a matter of "knowing" as it is "being" or "walking." We must learn to take hold of what God has provided for us and walk in His blessings by faith. Paul is a great "pray-er," and he gives us a wonderful example of a prayer that you and I can pray for ourselves and everyone we know.

H. A. Ironside, former pastor of the Moody Memorial Church in Chicago, gave this outline for Paul's prayer (with comments by the author):

- Verse 16, Endowment: God has provided everything we need.
- Verse 16, Enduement: God has given us the power we need.
- Verse 17, Enthronement: God dwells within us.
- Verse 17, Establishment: God roots and grounds us in Him.
- Verse 18, Enlightenment: God gives us the ability to comprehend spiritual insights.

- Verse 19, Enlargement: We can grow greater in our knowledge of God's love.
- Verse 19, Enrichment: We become spiritually richer as we surrender to God more. (See endnote 8).

We have to take hold with confidence and assertiveness, knowing indeed, who we are. Paul will amplify this in vv. 18-19. Note how Paul's prayer builds the 'inner man'. It would do each of us good to read his four prison prayers (Ephesians 1, here in cp. 3, and the other two in Philippians 1 and Colossians 1), and use each of them for our own prayers. Insert your name into the prayers. Pray the prayers for the one you desire to grow in Christ.

Paul picks up where he left off in v. 1, and the first thing we notice is his posture. Keep in mind, vv. 2-13 of cp. 3 are a parenthesis.

PAUL IN PRAYER

Verse 14 continues (actually picks up from v. 1). He uses the same words, **For this reason.** What reason? The Gentiles' *past*, now their *present* life through union with Christ. Paul is explaining the relationship.

We see Paul in prayer **I bow my knees before the Father of our Lord Jesus Christ**—down on his knees in honor as he prays to the Father. Regardless of Paul's physical position, he first reminds the Gentiles, by referring to **Father**, they are all part of God's family. Families should stick together and he is about to tell them how to do that. Paul had already prayed for them in Ephesians 1 when he emphasized they should *know* their inheritance in Christ. In this second prayer, he stresses how they should *live out* that inheritance.

We need to learn to spend time on our knees. Dare I say, too many of us, spend too little time . . . . down on our knees, for whatever the reason. I am guilty of this. That is where "fellowship" with God takes place. Oh, I plead with you . . . . get down! Get under . . . get low . . . . get submissive before Him!

Someone said, *"No man is as tall, as when he is on his knees"*

Think about Paul's position—on his knees, **I bow my knees**. That position was very unusual in Paul's day.

The people in his day usually stood. The priests—stood tall, to be seen. To kneel was only out of urgency or deep adoration.

There are several positions for prayer mentioned in the Bible. Abraham **stood** before the Lord in Genesis 18:22, as did Solomon in 1 Kings 8:22. David **sat** before the Lord in 1 Chronicles 17:16. Jesus **fell** *on His face* in the Garden (Matthew 26). Solomon (1 Kings 8:54), Elijah (1 Kings 18:42) and Daniel (Daniel 6:10) are shown *kneeling*. In Mark 11:25 and Luke 18:11 we see *standing* in prayer. We see *lifting* hands (1 Timothy 2:8 and Psalm 141:2), *bowing* (Genesis 24:26, Exodus 4:31; 34:8), *on one's face* (Numbers 20:6; Matthew 26:39), and *secret* prayer (Matthew 6:6; Acts 10:9; Luke 5:16). The humble spirit submits to God whether standing, lying, walking or bowing.

I notice that Paul places an emphasis on posture in Ephesians. **Buried** in spiritual death (2:1) at one time, and remember the words "but God" who **raised** us from the dead and **seated** us with Christ (2:4-6). Because of that, we now **walk** to please Him (4:1) and we will see later (6:10) we can **stand** against the devil. However, the posture that links "sitting" with "walking" and "standing" is "bowing."

This is his attitude as we continue Paul's thoughts here. It is one of deep honor, respect, and adoration—to the Father. *I bow my knees.* It must have been quite an experience for the Roman soldier who was chained to Paul most of the time. Is it any wonder that the whole prison guard and entire household of the prisoners, heard about Paul? At the time of Paul's house arrest for two years, the many visitors were greatly affected by this "arrangement."

We have here and elsewhere in the Bible, a picture of prayer that is always *addressed* to the Father, *through* the Son, and *in* the Spirit.

Paul begins in v. 16 a prayer, which includes all of us. This is our prayer for all Christians. He said in [15] ***every family in heaven and on earth.*** He includes *four specific requests.* Moreover, these are not four *separate or individual* petitions. They are not *only* a list, but also what we could describe as similar to a pyramid of requests. The prayer is an outline of what to pray; each step includes a higher walk in Christ. One is given, and the next builds on it, and the next builds on the last one, building towards a climax! Actually, these requests are additional, wonderful benefits/ blessings that you and I are to pray for and receive. We saw nine of them in cp. 1.

Many of us have heard the old saying "His benefits are out of this world!" A truthful play on words making it clear that all the many benefits/blessings of God originate from the Father in heaven.

The **first** request: We are **STRENGTHENED THROUGH HIS SPIRIT**

He says: [16] *to be strengthened and reinforced with mighty power in the inner man by the [Holy] Spirit [Himself indwelling your innermost being and personality].*

What a great verse for each one of us to pray. Oh my! Go to Him and say *"God strengthen me, reinforce me with your mighty power . . . . be strong in me Holy Spirit . . . . fuse in my personality".*

The dispenser of the power of God is the Holy Spirit. This power only comes by feeding on the Word, by breathing the pure air of prayer, and exercising daily service for God. Later, we will see when studying about the armor, that this is related to "taking the sword *of* the Spirit."

We do not have space, nor is it our purpose to present a deep teaching on the Holy Spirit. I suggest you read the book of Acts and notice the importance of the Holy Spirit in the life of the Church. There are at least fifty-nine references to the Spirit in Acts, 25% of the total references in the New Testament to the Holy Spirit. The true Christian cannot ignore the place the Holy Spirit has within the inner man.

A sad comment from one unknown teacher: *"If God took the Holy Spirit out of this world, most of what we Christians are doing would go right on—and nobody would know the difference!"* This is certainly quite sad, but perhaps true. Make a commitment to listen to the Spirit. Learn how to recognize His voice.

May I just suggest we use the word "Christian" less and less? You and I are, or should be, beyond the world's understanding of Christian. Many who call themselves "Christian" are not true believers who know and stand in their redemption and their place in Christ. I like to refer to the term "believers"; true believers in all that we are *in Christ*.

This bears repeating: The inner man is the spirit-man. Every one of us has "an inner man". In fact, we could say, each of us *is* this inner person, this inner man.

Concerning the inner man, Romans 7:22 says, *delights in the law of God*. This is the one renewed day by day and is built up to wage warfare! ¹⁶ **To be strengthened and reinforced with mighty power in the inner man by the [Holy] Spirit.**

The Bible says that even though the outer body is perishing, the inner man is being renewed! Each one of us faces difficulties in our life-walk. Sufferings, caused by the trinity of three forces (the world, the flesh, and the devil) coming against us. Therefore, Paul prays that we can be strengthened by the power of the Holy Spirit as we face many obstacles. We need a helper as we face temptations, worries, and fears. Paul prays here, for us to know the *pneuma, Christ's very spirit, the Holy Spirit*. This One comforts and counsels each believer.

> Then a second request from Paul in his prayer: Pray to be **THE DWELLING PLACE OF CHRIST** ¹⁷ *May Christ through your faith [actually] dwell (settle down, abide, make His permanent home) in your hearts!*

Of course we know Jesus takes up residence in a person at the time of conversion (John 14:23). This is not the subject in this prayer. This is not a question of His being *in* the believer, but rather of His feeling *at home* there.

ASK: *Is He made welcome in my heart?*

Have you ever visited someone in his or her home, and just did not feel welcome? Perhaps you felt uncomfortable or tense during the visit? If that has ever been your experience, you probably never wanted to return!

The heart is the center of your *life* and controls every aspect of existence. Should we not make Jesus welcome there? Should He not be taken in to every room of our life? Do not allow Him to be shut out of any secrete chambers within. Allow Him freedom to walk in to every compartment.

Pray to Him, love Him, and welcome Him. Make your heart a welcome residence for Him.

Paul uses this word ***dwell***. The AMP Bible that we are using describes it perfectly from the Greek word, which means *to settle down, abide, and feel at home.*

Paul is yearning for Christ to be welcome *in* your heart, not be a surface relationship, rather an ever-deepening fellowship. The meaning here goes deeper. Paul uses a word that could be interpreted as "one becoming the owner." Christ is to be welcomed yes, but also acknowledged as the "Head" of the household. We too often have missed this truth.

A third part of Paul's prayer: **ROOTED IN LOVE.** #1 **STRENGTHENED THROUGH HIS SPIRIT,** #2 **A DWELLING PLACE OF CHRIST,** and now #3 **ROOTED IN LOVE**.

¹⁷ᵇ *May you be rooted deep in love and founded securely on love.*

The word "rooted" brings to mind plants with roots shooting deep into the earth—a botanical word. We have to "dig deeper' or "go down" into the soil of fellowship with Christ. Dig in and tap into His love reservoir of *spiritual sap*.

Think of the tree in Psalm 1. We are to be . . . *like a tree firmly planted by the streams of water, ready to bring forth its fruit in its season; its leaf also shall not fade or wither; and everything he does shall prosper*

In v. 17 the words *founded securely* are similar, but are more related to a foundation. Our very foundation is Christ's love. *Founded* is an architectural term referring to that foundation.

So *rooted* nourishes us, *founded* establishes our solidity and longevity.

Jesus taught us about the importance of the foundation, in Matthew 7. The storm that blows reveals the strength and depth of the foundation. Foundations may stand firm, weaken, of fall down as winds and storms "blow" past your life.

Paul continues in v. 18 and the first part of v. 19 with his reasoning.
¹⁸ *That __you__ may have the power and be strong to __apprehend__ and __grasp__ with all the saints [God's devoted people, the experience of that love] what is the breadth and length and height and depth [of it]; ¹⁹ᵃ [That you may really come] to know [practically, through experience for yourselves] the*

love of Christ, which far surpasses mere knowledge [without experience]. (Underlines added for emphasis)

The English words *apprehend and grasp* are strong words. They describe mentally taking hold of something. On the other hand, it is possible to have understanding, and then *not take it* for yourself. You have heard this said, "I know that I know that I know"—not profound, but good advice.

The words *apprehend and grasp* amplify the single word in the Greek; the meaning includes "laying hold of what is being said" *but also includes* to "possess it as your own." An additional meaning is "to take hold and win the trophy by obtaining it."

Just a note here: Jesus said something very important in Matthew 6:31 *Therefore take no thought, saying,*

A thought may come, but you do not have to "take it."

"I'm afraid of that"

"Scared to death"

"That'll never happen"

"I always get the flu"

Thoughts *can* be cast down! Paul suggests what thoughts to "take" in Philippians 4:8 *Finally, brethren, whatever is true, whatever is honorable, whatever is right, whatever is pure, whatever is lovely, whatever is of good repute, if there is any excellence and if anything worthy of praise, dwell on these things.*

Remember, thoughts that are released through your own words are dropped into the heart. So use your voice to take hold and grasp Paul's thoughts.

Paul's concern was that we lay hold of the vast expanse of the love of God. "Take hold" in this four-fold dimension thought: [18b] *the breadth and length and height and depth [of it].* We are to be aware of the extent of God's love in the many routine persecutions of life. I like what Stott says: *the love of Christ is 'broad' enough to encompass all mankind (especially Jew and Gentiles, the theme of these chapters), 'long' enough to last for eternity, 'deep' enough to reach the most degraded sinner, and 'high' enough to exalt him to heaven."*[23]

I think of another *unnamed* prisoner who wrote of God's love. It was found penciled on the wall of a patient's room in an insane asylum:

> *Could we with ink the oceans fill*
> *And were the skies of parchment made,*
> *Were every stalk on earth a quill*
> *And every man a scribe by trade*
> *To write the love of God above*
> *Would drain the oceans dry;*
> *Nor could the scroll contain the whole*
> *Though stretched from sky to sky.*

Here is a paradox: Paul wanted us to know personally that the love of Christ ***far surpasses mere knowledge.*** There are dimensions that cannot be measured: ***the love of Christ, which far surpasses mere knowledge.*** We are so rich in Christ that our riches cannot be calculated, even though Paul has attempted to inform us. Remember those times when Paul in writing floats away in jubilation to Christ?

The fourth part of Paul's prayer, **FILLED WITH GOD'S OWN FULLNESS**

Continuing, 19b ***that you may be filled [through all your being] unto all the fullness of God [may have the richest measure of the divine Presence, and become a body wholly filled and flooded with God Himself]!***

We see yet another time where God's greatness overwhelms Paul, as it should overwhelm us. He turns *his own* eyes away from himself, and *our* eyes away from us, to the only One who deserves glory.

God wants us to experience His fullness; ***that you may be filled unto all the fullness of God.*** The *means* of our fullness is the Holy Spirit (Ephesians 5:18), and the *measure* of our fullness is God Himself (Ephesians 4:11-16). Do not measure yourself by the weakest Christian that you know, and then boast, "I'm better than that one." We tend to compare ourselves with others. This is a false picture.

In this first area of study, **The Position of The Believer**, we have seen that *positionally* we are complete in Him; that is grace by faith. However, we will see in the next area, there is also a *practical* fullness.

Paul's benediction is vv. 20-21. Paul has prayed concerning the wonderful position we have **in Christ** and then continues forth with a great conclusion. Again, notice the Trinity. Paul prays to the **Father** concerning the indwelling power of God the **Spirit**, made available through God the **Son.**

> Here is another of the great verses to read over and over in our devotions: [20] *Now to Him Who, by (in consequence of) the [action of His] power that is at work within us, is able to [carry out His purpose and] do superabundantly, far over and above all that we [dare] ask or think [infinitely beyond our highest prayers, desires, thoughts, hopes, or dreams]—*[21] *To Him be glory in the church and in Christ Jesus throughout all generations forever and ever. Amen (so be it).*

Paul exhausted every word possible to explain the vastness of God's power as found in Christ. What more explanation could be offered than our God who does **far over and above all** we even think or dream about? Notice He **is able**. What confidence this should build in each of us. He is able! In addition, He is not asleep or unconcerned. He is active to **do superabundantly.** The Greek explains He is able to perform and create. He *is able*, and *He does* what is needed for each of His children. Also, notice we are to **ask.** We do not have to back away from asking. This should *also* be a comfort. Not only is He able and a doer, He is a super listener! Talk to Him. He loves you.

As we close Part One of Ephesians, our *Position in Christ*, reach out and receive your spiritual wealth by opening your heart to the Holy Spirit and praying with Paul for strength in the inner man. Pray . . .

- For a new depth of love
- For the help of the Holy Spirit

- For Christ to be welcome in you
- For a continuous fullness of God

Let's get overwhelmed with Him! Remind yourself of the final five Psalms which begin and end with *"Praise Him," "Praise Him."*

Section Four
Additional Questions and Thoughts for Discussion

1. What is Paul's 'mystery' that he describes?
2. What is the significance today of Jews and Gentiles as being one body?
3. Discuss H.A. Ironside's outline for Paul's second prayer.
4. How will you change your prayer life comparing your past prayers with Paul's prayer?
5. Discuss the Holy Spirit and His help in your prayer life.
6. What is being 'rooted and grounded' in love?
7. Discuss Paul's four requests in his prayer.

Part Two

THE PRACTICE OF THE BELIEVER

ELEVEN

Body Parts Working In Unity

We come to a new emphasis in Paul's writing. Let's review where we are in Ephesians.

You might want to review the Outline in the first chapter of our study. The first three chapters of Ephesians examined **The Position of the Believer**. In those chapters, we looked at four sections that were a progression of Paul's teaching:

The Believer's Riches In Christ
The Believer's Enlightenment
The Believer's Victory
The Believer's Maturity

Paul wrote *doctrine* on several important areas: Predestination, election, adoption, redemption and the Holy Spirit. Now he begins the *practical* results of doctrine.

That first part of our course taught about an exalted place for every believer. It was as though we were lying in the cool grass or beside a flowing brook, listening for three chapters in Ephesians. Now it is time to get up, realize our position, and practice what we have learned—*walk*! *Knowledge must be followed by equal action.*

D. Martyn Lloyd-Jones describes this principle as a scale on which the weight placed on one side equals the weight on the opposite side. Believers must balance out their life by placing the knowledge learned on equal footing with their action. If your nature is to be *active*, perhaps you act without receiving *knowledge*. You might do a lot of reading and studying, and not following it with action.

Chapter 4 in Ephesians marks a definite break in Ephesians.

We move to the godly conduct of believers, which is the normal result of those first ten chapters of this course. We move *from* **The Position,** *to* **The Practice of the Believer.** This is the practical part of a believer's life. The *position* calls for a corresponding *conduct.* We will review this area in *four* sections:

> Unity of Believers
> Morality of Believers
> Life at Home and Work for The Believer
> Warfare and the Believer.

Each of Paul's letters contains a beautiful balance between doctrine and duty. Ephesians is a perfect example of that. He dealt in the first three chapters of Ephesians with doctrine. This revealed our *riches* in Christ. These last three chapters of Ephesians will explain our *duty and responsibility* in Christ.

The key word in the first three chapters was *wealth,* what we gained and received by being **in Christ**. The key word in the last three chapters is *walk.* Paul says walk in *unity* (cp. 4), walk in *purity* (5a), walk in *harmony* (5b), and concludes with a walk in *victory* (6).

The first section in part two is vv. 1-16 of Ephesians cp. 4. It is entitled **The Unity of Believers.** We will look at the topic by dividing it into two paragraphs, the first one being vv. 1-6 and entitled **Body Parts Working in Unity.**

We begin in v. 1 as Paul for the second time refers to himself as a **prisoner**. This time He refers to himself as **the prisoner for the Lord.** Showing the consistency of the Holy Spirit's writing, he combines the **prisoner** and the **servant** that we saw in cp. 3. Paul counts this as an honor, **the prisoner for the Lord**. The rest of the world might call it 'disgraceful'—a prisoner of a dead person (Christ)!

However, Paul is imprisoned as a result of faithfulness and obedience to deliver his assignment (his message to the Gentiles). That assignment did not lead him to a sandy beach or a nice resort area—it led him to a literal prison. [1] *I THEREFORE, the prisoner for the Lord.*

He encourages his readers *to walk (lead a life) worthy of the [divine] calling to which you have been called*

He does not command them, rather he appeals to them in words and attitude of grace.

This word *walk* is found seven times in Ephesians. It describes a person's entire lifestyle, not a physical walk, although that indeed is included. This is a walk of their new life *in Christ* that is consistent with their **POSITION** in the Body of Christ. Paul also adds the word *worthy*, meaning "equal to." The knowledge of the position *and* the walking *in* that knowledge are given equal importance by Paul.

A LIFE IN CHRIST

As we continue in v. 2, we will see the believer is to show a Christ-like spirit in every area of life. I will say that *not a single one of these is easy!* Again, I mention it: We can learn many things about our position in Christ, but the knowledge will be of little assistance in a victorious life if the instructions are not *lived*. The *walk* or *life-style* *in Christ* is to consist of four specific areas:

#1 **Lowliness,** [2] *Living as becomes you with complete lowliness of mind (humility)*

This is a genuine humility that can only come from closeness to the Lord. This humility is the opposite of pride. The more we realize our **Position** with Him, the more we are able to walk in humility *with* Him. It cannot happen without being in fellowship with Christ. Normally we like to get our own way. Come on now . . . . admit it! Paul in this first life-style suggests the opposite approach: Go against the normal or natural reaction to life. Paul is certain that God is calling all believers to be God-like in all relationships. Paul directs his readers to face this life-style of *lowliness.* Notice, he says this after writing about the high position and blessings we mentioned, perhaps to remind them not to be "puffed up."

Humbleness makes us conscious of our own nothingness. This is not meaning we are nothing—far be it from that. We have many benefits, but indeed, it is with humility. Humbleness is also the opposite of conceit and arrogance. Paul says in Philippians 2:3 . . . . *Instead, in the true spirit of humility (lowliness of mind) let each regard the others as better than and superior to himself [thinking more highly of one another than you do of yourselves].*

Humility is essential to Paul's whole theme here of "unity" in this Section. It marks a follower of Christ as much as when Christ washed the feet of His friends.

It is an attitude of the heart that recognizes Christ first, others and their needs next, and self last!

Christ wants us to know our benefits, and not to think *more highly* of ourselves. On the other hand, do not think *less highly*. Are you with me?

> #2 Our life is also one of **Gentleness.** Follow our Scripture here [2] *Living as becomes you with complete lowliness of mind (humility) <u>and</u> meekness (unselfishness, gentleness, mildness).* (Underline added for emphasis)

Gentleness certainly goes hand in hand with **Lowliness** (humility).

This is changing our attitude to submit to God's leadership without rebellion. It is seen in Jesus as He said, *"I am gentle and <u>lowly in heart"</u>* in Matthew 11:29. We read that Moses was a meek man in Numbers 12:3. I love Philippians 2:5 *Let this same <u>attitude </u> and purpose and [humble] mind be in you which was in Christ Jesus.* (Underline added for emphasis)

Think about Jesus, the One who made the worlds, who flung the stars into space and calls each of them by name. He is the One who preserves the innumerable constellations in their courses. He is the One who maintains it all, holding it all together by His Word. When He comes into human life, He is described as a *gentle lamb*! (Jeremiah 11:19). This is not a weakness by any means. Jesus and Moses, were gentle and meek men, but very strong! There is no weakness here. *Knowing* what we have in those first three chapters we studied—and *now walking* in humbleness and gentleness. This is not easy or normal in our world. The Greek language uses this word as a *soothing medicine,* a *colt that has been broken,* and as a *soft wind.* Each carries the meaning of "power under control." Each is **gentleness.** *It is not a power of control.*

> **A third** lifestyle or walk is **With Patience.** Again read [2] *Living as becomes you with complete lowliness of mind (humility) and meekness (unselfishness, gentleness, mildness), with patience.*

So #1 a *lowliness* in heart, #2 a *gentleness* in attitude, and now #3 doing it all with *patience.* I told you none of this was easy!

Lowliness (humility) is the hardest of these traits, but **patience** comes in the hardest way.

Think of this as having an "even disposition" no matter what comes! Endure without striking back! Wow. I have not yet mastered this *life part* of the walk yet.

This is similar to the little puppy that barks at the big dog. The big dog could snap and bite at the little one, but generally "puts up" with him. Perhaps you have seen something similar with dogs and little infants. When my daughter was young, she would pull and pull our poodle's ears, but "Mimi" never snapped back. She just endured. This is how *patience* is to work.

The Scripture goes on . . . *bearing with one another and making allowances because you love one another.*

We really could also call this trait "tolerance"—the making of allowance for the faults and failures of others. Wouldn't it be a great world, if we just followed these life-styles we are reviewing in Ephesians cp. 4?

Notice the pathway to patience: *because you love one another.* There are four words for love in the Greek language (three used in the New Testament). The love between men and women including sexual happenings is *eros.* The love of friends is *philia.* Another, *storqe* is love between family members. Then the well-known word, *agape* is the God kind of love. Paul uses *this* word in our Scripture. God wants to bless His children and love them with no motive in mind. He wants what is best for the individual. I see the first three words involving a *feeling,* but the fourth is a *decision,* which may or may not involve feelings.

We also realize from Romans 5:3 *Moreover [let us also be full of joy now!] let us exult and triumph in our troubles and rejoice in our sufferings, knowing that pressure and affliction and hardship produce patient and unswerving endurance.*

Difficulties in life, tribulations during our walk, *will* come. Walking through them in love *will* grow patience.

Then another lifestyle of these *in Christ*. #4: **Preserve Unity**

> ³ **Be eager and strive earnestly to guard and keep the harmony and oneness of [and produced by] the Spirit in the binding power of peace.**

Paul's emphasis over the next thirteen verses is unity because of its great importance.

When God formed the Church, he eliminated the greatest division that had every existed: The rift we studied earlier between Jews and Gentiles.

So *in Christ*, the distinctions between Jews and Gentiles were abolished. However, a question remained unanswered: Would it work out in real life? Was Church unity just "an idea," only a "dream" or "hope?" Perhaps there would be a "Jewish Church of Christ" and a "Church of All Nations." Would it work? Therefore, Paul tries to guard against any division, pleading for unity among the entire body.

To keep the **oneness of the Spirit** is to realize the Holy Spirit has made all true believers one *in Christ*. This is the character of the Church. Every member is to be like Christ, wanting what God wants and not what the individual wants.

This is a unity nothing can destroy. However, on earth, we *strive* to live at peace with one another! Ironic. Unity is what binds members together in spite of national or religious differences. This is the only hope our nation has to live in world prominence. This is the result of Isaiah 7:14.

What a lesson to live by!

Paul amplifies this life style using the word **one**. The Church is one body—each part working for the good of the whole. I like to use the physical body to picture this unity. Each "part," the leg, arm, foot, hand, mouth, ear, etc. work towards the same goal. What if your hand and arm grab hold of the mailbox, while your foot and leg wanted to get in your car? Division! Instead of magnifying differences, we should think of the next *seven positive* realities, which form our Christian unity. What follows is a seven-fold fullness of *unity*.

> He says in describing unity: [4] *[There is] one body and one Spirit-just as there is also one hope [that belongs] to the calling you received—*[5] *[There is] one Lord, one faith, one baptism,* [6] *one God and Father of [us] all, Who is above all [Sovereign over all], pervading all and [living] in [us] all.*

"one body"

Body is a metaphor for Church. This of course is the body of Christ in which every believer is a member. He or she was placed there at conversion by the Holy Spirit. This refers to a Living Body, which grows by multiplication of cells. I mentioned body and cells in previous comments. Paul mentions this in 1 Corinthians 12:25-27 **So that there should be no division or discord or lack of adaptation [of the parts of the body to each other], but the members all alike should have a mutual interest in and care for one another.** [26] **And if one member suffers, all the parts [share] the suffering; if one member is honored, all the members [share in] the enjoyment of it.** [27] **Now you [collectively] are Christ's body and [individually] you are members of it, each part severally and distinct [each with his own place and function].**

In spite of differences in race, color, nationality, culture, language or temperament, there is one body, made up of all believers, from Pentecost to Rapture.

We need to wipe away all 'tags'. However, being one body does not prevent each member from finding and being a part of a local church.

"one Spirit"

This word is capitalized, and rightly so. The same Holy Spirit dwells in every believer and is what proves we belong to each other in the Lord. The same Holy Spirit dwells inside the Body of Christ, producing and yearning unity. The Church is *one* because of the work of the **one Spirit.**

No doubt, a purpose of His entering into every individual and fellowshipping with each one is to mold unity. The filling of the Holy Spirit certainly assists in producing "oneness."

The book of Ephesians has a number of references to the Holy Spirit; I found at least ten. He is so important in this subject of unity. I suggest you look for Him and perhaps "code" those in your own personal way, perhaps by marking each reference in blue.

#3 Paul adds *"one hope"* of your calling

Our English word "hope" has lost its meaning in our day. Today we use the word as defining an uncertainty. It may also refer to a possibility in the future, but not expected. However, our Scripture refers directly to the return of Jesus to take His Church to heaven. The Holy Spirit within the believer is that assurance. We mentioned this in cp. 1.

Paul refers to *hope* as something that should unite the Church. We speak of a doctrine called eschatology—the many events of the last days. These events would include Tribulation, Millennium and judgments. However when considering these events, little unity of this hope exists. Therefore, the detail or specifics of all last day events, is not a unifying doctrine. However, we must understand every member of the Body of Christ is called to one destiny—to be with Christ, to be like Him, and to share His Glory, endlessly! We all have this common, single *hope*. We share the same future. Of course, this one hope certainly includes a walk as a peacemaker of v. 3.

> Paul says *"one Lord."* This of course is our Lord Jesus Christ who *died* for us, *lives* for us, and is *coming* for us. Acknowledging the Lordship of Christ is the only thing that could ever bring unity. The first three unities are the work of the Holy Spirit. These next three are joined around Christ.

Someone asked Ghandi "What is the greatest hindrance to Christianity in India?" Anyone want to guess His reply? Take a wild guess—the answer can be found later.[24] There is no doubt as to what makes a genuine Christian: Believing in, receiving, and living for Christ. Christ is the *"one Lord."*

1 Corinthians 8:5-6 ***For although there may be so-called gods, whether in heaven or on earth, as indeed there are many of them, both of gods and of lords and masters,*** [6] ***Yet for us there is [only] one God, the Father, Who is the Source of all things and for Whom we [have life], and one Lord, Jesus Christ, through and by Whom are all things and through and by Whom we [ourselves exist].***

There are not many Lords. Every believer has to walk in **one Lord**. Acknowledge Him and walk as one.

> Also, there's **"one faith"** listed here. This is our Christian Faith. There is one body of Truth. This is the faith of all believers, unified together in One Body, the Church. Jude [3] **the faith which was once for all handed down to the saints**. Christians may differ in some matters, but all true believers agree on "the faith," and to depart from **one faith** would bring disunity in the body. Yes, we are saved by our faith, but Paul refers to this unified faith of all believers.

The early Church recognized a body of basic doctrine, which they guarded and taught (2 Timothy 2:2).

We never depart from "the faith," which helps bring us into unity.

> #6 is **"one baptism."** There are several different commentations on this, making this an unusual unity to be included. It can divide a local church even though it is to unify. Ironic.

I do not see any teaching by Paul in the *method* of baptism. Therefore, we can safely remove this from being a reference to water baptism. Water baptism does identify one with Christ, but the context of Paul's letter is much deeper.

Since Paul was discussing the unified body and has taught throughout Ephesians concerning a new birth, this *baptism* is most likely the Holy Spirit baptizing a person *into Christ*. This is confirming again and emphasizing the oneness, the unity of Jews and Gentiles into the Church. Romans 6:3 says ***Are you ignorant of the fact that all of us who have been baptized into Christ Jesus . . .***

In addition, we will see in 5:18 another possible relationship to baptism; we are commanded to be ***filled and stimulated*** with the Spirit.

> Paul's seven-fold fullness of *unity* is concluded in verse ⁶ "***One God and Father" of [us] all, Who is above all [Sovereign over all], pervading all and [living] in [us] all.***

> ***One God.*** The first three centered around the Holy Spirit, the next three around Jesus Christ, and now the final one centers on God the Father.

Several times Paul emphasized God as Father in this letter: 1:3, 17; 2:18; 3:14 and 5:20.

He makes it clear to us: The Father is ***above all,*** the supreme Sovereign of the universe

He acts *through* all the body, using everyone and everything, to accomplish His purposes.

He is in every believer, present in all places, at the same instant! Another fact I cannot get my thinking around.

As I was preparing this paragraph, I thought of Colossians 1:15-18:

¹⁵ ***[Now] He is the exact likeness of the unseen God [the visible representation of the invisible]; He is the Firstborn of all creation.*** ¹⁶ ***For it was in Him that all things were created, in heaven and on earth, things seen and things unseen, whether thrones, dominions, rulers, or authorities; all things were created and exist through Him [by His service, intervention] and in and for Him.*** ¹⁷ ***And He Himself existed before all things, and in Him all things consist (cohere, are held together).*** ¹⁸ ***He also is the Head of [His] body, the church; seeing He is the Beginning, the Firstborn from among the dead, so that He alone in everything and in every respect might occupy the chief place [stand first and be preeminent].***

TWELVE

Use Your Gifts

We continue in Ephesians cp. 4, with v. 7. Paul seems to suddenly stop in his thoughts. He moves from what *all believers* have in common, all the *"oneness"* or *unity* we reviewed in the previous chapter (ELEVEN), to the *variety* of gifts He gives to individual members. An entire book could be written on these next few verses. Several commentators believe these verses are the heart of the entire book. However, there is certainly no consensus as to exact interpretation. Verse 7 reads **Yet grace was given to <u>each</u> of us <u>individually</u> [not indiscriminately, but in different ways] in proportion to the measure of Christ's [rich and bounteous] gift.** (Underline added for emphasis)

Paul affirms here that every member of God's body was given grace. I like to say, "Jesus graced us" (we *are* saved by His grace). We can also note that every believer, *each of us individually* has been given at least one gift. There are many gifts in the Scriptures: 1 Corinthians 12:8-10, 28-30; Romans 12:6-8; Ephesians 4:11 and 1 Peter 4:11. Read them, study them, see if you recognize your gifting. I would suggest the following method to discover your gift (s):

1. Begin with a study of the various gifts (in the five lists reference above). Do not resist any one of them—remain open as you learn about each.

2. Pray concerning the gifts. God may speak to your heart about something that you would not consider on your own. Do not resist

what He places before you. What He has for you is much better than what you naturally desire.

3. Assess your abilities and strengths. This in itself will not determine your gift (s), however could be an indication of such.

This grace of v. 7 is not *only* saving grace; although *it's by grace we are saved*. (Ephesians 2:5). The context we are studying in 4:7 is God's grace in granting multiple gifts to His children.

Paul wrote earlier about the unity of the body, the "oneness"; now he says Jesus gave *out of His immeasurable grace* various blessings to the individuals *in* the body. This is what produces the unity of the Church.

These gifts included different ways for every believer to mature within the body. There are many "gifts" in this "gift."

- Christ *Himself* is of course the ***unspeakable gift*** (2 Corinthians 9:15) KJV
- Paul wrote about *Christ our peace* in Ephesians 3
- The *Holy Spirit* is a gift to believers
- *Salvation,* which we mentioned, is a gift
- *Eternal Life*
- *Spiritual* gifts

In reality, *all good things* are His gifts

Therefore, the ***gift*** of v. 7 is not the ***gifts*** we will visit in v. 8.

Paul is saying every believer has received grace. He saved you. Everyone accepting Him is in His body. You have been given a place. Christ is *full* of grace and He portioned out of this grace, a grace to every one of us. Continuing forward from His unity theme, the part of the body each is to occupy is assigned, in proportion ***to the measure of Christ's gift.*** (I remind you to review the four Scriptures concerning the variety of gifts than His Body has been given).

Paul continues by saying that He gave some ***gifts***, to help this body of believers to mature [8b] ***and He bestowed gifts on men.*** In fact, He arose on Easter morning and later ascended to heaven as a conqueror *for* His body, and placed these specific leadership *gifts* to help that body. Christ gives out of Himself, out of His grace, a gift with various acts, to His "body parts." Individuals have many gifts given by His full-grace, *but* some *specific* individuals have a leadership assignment (Paul told us about *his own* assignment to the Gentiles).

Paul paints us a picture here of a military conqueror leading his captives and sharing the spoil. In this event, the captivity took place in a chamber described as *Abraham's bosom* or *Paradise.* No one in Paradise could have been saved before the blood of Christ was shed and sprinkled over an altar. The Old Testament saints were in Paradise. Jesus also visited the *other side* of the lower earth that was separate from Paradise. There He faced Satan and all his angels, defeated them along with death itself.

Paul uses David's experience from Psalm 68:18 that he paraphrases and applies to Christ.

Verse 18 in that Psalm reads ***Therefore it is said, When He ascended on high, He led captivity captive [He led a train of vanquished foes] and He bestowed gifts on men.***

> Going on, Paul uses that event and tells us how David's military experience was fulfilled in Christ: [9] ***[But He ascended?] Now what can this, He ascended, mean but that He had previously descended from [the heights of] heaven into [the depths], the lower parts of the earth?***

What a statement! Keeping it in context—Jesus came to earth, went to a cross, descended to a lowest part of earth, took the Old Testament saints to heaven, and defeated Satan.

Now, let me paint you a picture, *a chronological journey* "From the Agony of the Cross, to the Triumph of the Throne." [25] Few seem to compile the time-line for these most-important events. In fact, I have read it only once or twice in my ministry. Therefore, travel with me, using abbreviated phrases, to a place where many "fear to tread!" When I taught this recently, a man said, "In all my fifty years in leadership, I have never heard such a clear explanation of these events."

We generally hear the short, incomplete version: *Jesus went to a cross, His body placed in a tomb; He rises on Sunday morning, appears to many, and ascends to heaven.* Let me fill in some details.

The chronological picture shows us Jesus . . .

On The Cross

Luke 23:44, darkness enveloped the whole land; creation went into mourning for the Substitute (Christ).

Matthew 27:51-54, an earthquake, shaking earth to the very center by the tragedy of Deity becoming humanity's Substitute.

Mathew 27:50-51, the veil of the temple was ripped and torn in two from top to bottom. Jehovah had moved out of the temple! The high priest and priesthood were no longer needed. They did not even realize it ended. Fifty years after this event, there was not one member of the high priestly family living, neither could one member of the Davidic line be found. There was no longer a Holy of Holies for the atonement blood to be sprinkled. Today the new creation, every believer, is God's temple (1 Corinthians 3:16).

Continuing On the cross:

Jesus *became* sin, He was a curse. The Father cannot look on sin, turns away from the Son. All types and forms of sin were loaded upon Him!

Isaiah 53:4-6, (also notice also v. 9) "death" is plural—Jesus died spiritually when He became sin. The sin then made His body mortal so He could die physically. A dual death.

Psalm 22 gives the graphic picture of the crucifixion of Jesus; written a thousand years before He hung on the cross, twenty years before crucifixion was practiced!

Jehovah had heard their cry and now delivers them.
He is becoming sin; He is spiritually dead, a worm.
Read John 3:14, Jesus became a serpent with Satan.
There was no one to help, the disciples were powerless.

Many laughed at Jesus. They mocked Him. The Sanhedrin and the Senate, the "bulls of Bashan" gape upon Him and crucify Him.
Jesus had died of a ruptured heart, John 19:31-35.
Every bone in His body crying out in agony.
The Roman soldier "dogs"—Jews always called them this.

They looked upon His nakedness—such humiliation.
The Psalmist had described it more accurately than any of the eyewitnesses.

It is finished, the Abrahamic Covenant was over. He was sin and was turned over to Satan by God.

Hebrews 8:1-13, tells of the New Covenant.
1 Peter tells of many new sacrifices that today we offer to the Father. Also Hebrews 13:15.

In Hell (Sheol, Heb; Hades, Gk)

Three days and three nights in hell, Matthew 12:40

When Jesus died, His spirit was taken by Satan to hell, the place where all sinners will go. Hell is simply the temporary county jail; the Lake of Fire is the Eternal Prison (no one is there yet). He went into dreaded regions and paid the penalty of our sinful nature.

Psalm 88 says He sank to the lowest depths of Hades. Notice this translation: *My life draws near to Sheol (the place of the dead); go down into the pit; You have laid me in the depths of the lowest pit, in darkness, in the deeps.* (AMP)

(There are many theologians or commentators who interpret the chronology differently: Jesus, living on earth, Bethlehem, dying on a cross and going back to heaven. They interpret Ephesians 4:9 as "the lower parts of the universe" or others, a paraphrase such as "Jesus descended to the lowest level, the earth."

Some attribute Psalm 88 and other Scriptures as applying to Jesus *on earth* and in a tomb, but not related to His visit to *lower earth*.

Returning to the time line, Jesus arrived on Satan's side of lower earth, and welcomed by all the demons of hell. Then, just as they thought they *had* Him, He turned on them, defeating every *form of* death. The Bible says He made a show of them openly! Similar to the picture of a military conqueror leading his captives and sharing the spoil with his followers. It also reminds us of the victory march of David after capturing and returning what belonged to Israel, the Ark of the Covenant (1 Chronicles 15:27-29).

1 Timothy 3:16: After God *justified and vindicated in the [Holy] Spirit* (He had suffered for all) and then made *Him alive in the spirit* (1 Peter 3:18), Jesus was *born again.* He had met the claims of Justice.

Colossians 2:15 gives a description of the battle that took place in Hades before Jesus rose from the dead. He *disarmed the principalities and powers.* Matthew 12:29 tells us that He went into the strong man's house and bound him.

After Jesus had been justified and made alive in spirit, He became Satan's master. Hebrews 2:14 tells us Jesus paralyzed the death dealing power of Satan. When he met John (later), He said in Revelation 1:18 *I am alive forevermore, and I have the keys of death and of Hades.* Jesus took the keys of Death and Hell.

The Resurrection

This is greatest event that ever took place. Christ arose from the captivity of Satan! He threw Himself from the principalities and the powers. He made a show of them in the presence of all hell. Colossians 2:15

He was made alive in hell, born of the Spirit. (Acts 13:33 *You are My Son; today I have begotten You),* arose in omnipotent strength, ascended up out of the darkness of Hell and entered back into His body, which was then filled with light and Immortality. Out of that dark tomb came the light of the ages. Hebrews 1:6, 8 are the Words of God that reached down and said it is enough.

During the Forty days

Hebrews 9:12 tells of the journey to heaven immediately after this resurrection. However, a very tender drama takes place just before He does.

In John 20:11—18 the tomb is empty, two angels are there. Jesus speaks to Mary: *Do not cling to Me [do not hold Me].* He had to take His blood, as High Priest into the Heavenly Holy of Holies, to make redemption. He was saying, "Mary I am going to take my blood in to the New Holy of Holies, sprinkle it on the mercy seat just as our High Priests have been dong once a year, but mine is going to be an eternal sacrifice. I am going to consummate your redemption. You do not know it Mary, but I died for your sins, I have put them away. When I come back, you can put your hands on me, you can touch me, you may know that I am flesh and blood, but now I am going to my Father." *And He was gone.*

Enters the Heavenly Holy of Holies as Lord High Priest with His blood, establishing the New Covenant. He sprinkled His blood on that altar. No longer would a High Priest do this on earth, no longer was there an earthly Holy of Holies.

(Hebrews 9:11-12, 15). Now the Old Testament Fathers were redeemed. They were in Paradise waiting for Him. The thief on the cross was also there waiting.

Now Jesus would keep his promise made to the thief on the cross. "I say unto you *Today*, you will be with me in Paradise" (literal translation, notice the placement of the comma.)

1 Peter 3:18-19 He returned to lower earth and preached the good news to those gathered in Paradise. He took captive those who were there, thus taking captivity, captive (Ephesians 4:8-9). He could not have done this before He carried His blood in to The Holy of Holies.

Hebrews 10:29-22 gives us a glimpse of the new Holy of Holies. We are invited to come with boldness before the Throne of Grace in Hebrews 4:16.

During the forty days, we see the additional events of Luke 24:13-35, John 20:19-29 and John 21.

Acts 1:9-11 Jesus and a 'cloud' of Old Testament saints go into Heaven. He took everyone to heaven who had trusted in the promise—from Adam to the thief on the cross.

Sat down with the Father, He rested; His work was over. Hebrews 1:3

MEN-GIFTS

We return to v.11 in our course, where Jesus gave four ministry offices, (some scholars use five), to expand, educate, and protect His New Body, His Church.

> [11]*And His gifts were [varied; He Himself appointed and gave men to us] some to be apostles (special messengers), some prophets (inspired preachers and expounders), some evangelists (preachers of the Gospel, traveling missionaries),*

some pastors (shepherds of His flock) and teachers. (Underline added for emphasis)

Apostles
Prophets
Evangelists
Pastors and Teachers

Again, there is no consensus on the first two of these men-gifts. Scholars have different opinions as to whether these first two offices are still active.

I am not going to address in detail each of these gifts. Certainly, the *ministry* of each gift must continue.

ASK: *Why would we have a problem with the offices or leader positions still being filled? Perhaps, in a different way?*

Note the **apostle** was appointed to *take a message*. In *that* sense, we all *share* this ministry. In the sense of New Testament apostles laying the foundation of the Church, naturally none of us could qualify. (Note that there were at least twenty-four New Testament apostles). Today an apostle is thought of as one who takes the message to a people and lays the foundation for a "local church." That ministry exists.

Prophets proclaimed the Word of God. That ministry certainly *must* exist today. Their prophecy is to "edify, encourage, and console." Prophecy has always carried a meaning, which included "speaking forth." Prophets were not "only forecasters."

We mentioned in Ephesians 2:20 that the "foundation of the apostles and prophets" is what the unity of all believers is built on.

The **pastors and teachers** complete these man-gifts. Since the word *some* is not repeated, this probably indicates a single office. In addition, since the teaching gift is mentioned in other Scriptures, we do not need to split the office here in order to protect the teachers. Elsewhere Pastors are referred to by other names including elders and overseers.

Verse 12 gives three reasons God had for giving these gifts of men to His body. Again, I see these as the importance for the continuation of the four offices. Paul gives the entire process:

¹² *His intention was the perfecting and the full equipping of the saints (His consecrated people), [that they should do] the work of ministering toward building up Christ's body (the church).*

#1 *the full equipping of the saints*

God gave ministers to the church, to equip the believers. The KJV uses "the perfecting."

The word *equip* in the Greek is "katartismos." William Barclay explains that **equipping** in Greek "is used in surgery for setting a broken limb or for putting a joint back into its place. In politics, it is used for bringing together opposing factions so that government can go on. In the New Testament it is used of mending nets (Mark 1:19), and of disciplining an offender until he is fit to take his place again within the fellowship of the Church (Galatians 6:1). The basic idea of the word is that of putting a thing into the condition in which it ought to be."²⁶

"Equipping" or "perfecting" are both good translations from the Greek. Pastors and ministers teach and assist in maturing believers in order to present God's blessings to others.

> #2 *that they should do] the work of ministering* (or to be clearer, to do the work of serving.)

The *men-gifts* serve in their ministry, and by their example, *we too* are to be servants. Again, I confirm, all of us have a contribution and if we work together, we will accomplish the tasks at hand. You and I should welcome the training of our *spiritual overseers*. The goal is maturing into true servants of Christ. Use your abilities, allow them to be improved— and then do what you can in ministry to help others.

#3 *building up Christ's body*

This is really the goal. Build up His Church by caring and showing love, and by reaching out to a community with that same love and energy. Earlier Paul used the foundation of a building as an example of Christ.

Now he alludes to how a building is constructed. We as believers, part of the household of faith, are being constructed and matured.

> Verse 13 answers the question "how long will this process continue?" *[That it might develop] until we all attain oneness in the faith and in the comprehension of the [full and accurate] knowledge of the Son of God, that [we might arrive] at really mature manhood (the completeness of personality which is nothing less than the standard height of Christ's own perfection), the measure of the stature of the fullness of the Christ and the completeness found in Him.*

This can only happen when Jesus takes His Church home to heaven and we all arrive at this—*completeness found in Him.*

Until then, we will continue to have different views on many issues. However, the Church is to work together and allow the nature of Christ to blend into each of us. Someday we will understand the many questions we seem to strive with—perhaps we will not even want the answers! When God says in Revelation 21:5 *I make all things new*, the new will include memories.

We will mature fully one day ¹³ **in *the measure of the stature of the fullness of the Christ***

> ¹⁴ *So then, we may no longer be <u>children</u>, tossed [like ships] <u>to and fro</u> between chance gusts of teaching and wavering with every changing wind of doctrine, [the prey of] the cunning and cleverness of unscrupulous men, [gamblers engaged] in every shifting form of trickery <u>in inventing errors to mislead</u>.* (Underlines added for emphasis)

As long as we are active for Christ, praying, seeking, disciplining, and following His Word, we avoid three dangers listed here:

> **#1 Immaturity.** Remaining a spiritual child. It is vital to nourish those coming to Christ. Too many believers are undeveloped because of a lack of *spiritual exercise*—**Children.** I am quite sure we have fifty-year-old children in the body of Christ.

#2 Instability. Do not allow yourself to be susceptible to the "spiritual fads" that come along—professional quacks! Do not get misled into moving ***to and fro*** from one doctrine to another.

I strongly believe in a Foundations Course for all believers.[9] We must be solid in our walk with Him. Our foundation allows our life to stand in the storms that come.

#3 Gullibility. Deception is the most dangerous of the three. This is continuing weak in faith to the point of being unable to sense right and wrong, good and bad ***inventing errors to mislead.***

Verses 15-16 describe the proper practice for the Body of Christ. That is why I interpret the various and *different parts* of His gift of grace containing salvation, healing, the Holy Spirit, redemption, etc. Our life requires a maturity in all the doctrines.

> [15] ***Rather, let our lives lovingly express truth [in all things, speaking truly, dealing truly, living truly]. Enfolded in love, let us grow up in every way and in all things into Him Who is the Head, [even] Christ (the Messiah, the Anointed One).***

First, the Bible says ***let our lives lovingly express <u>truth.</u>*** Most versions say ***speaking the truth***.

Correct doctrine is vital. Your words must speak truth. I mentioned above that, I believe in a set of *statements of doctrine* based on Truth—those statements or foundations never change. There can be no compromise in fundamentals of truth. Note that v. 15 is more than doctrine—your whole life should be truth.

Second, speaking ***the truth . . . . in love.*** This is having a right spirit. The truth must be given in love and be expressed in a loving manner. It is a "body" of truth.

To walk any other way, is self-centered. Too many times, we express opinions or even spiritual truth as some special "herald of news" to others. Let's concentrate on our compassion and patience with everyone. Perhaps you are like me in this area. An incorrect attitude, method, or word sometimes defeats the love that is intended.

We also notice in v. 15, Paul again has the Church body in mind as he refers to **Him Who is the Head, [even] Christ (the Messiah, the Anointed One).**

Truth is the element in which we are to live, move, and have our being—But truth must be inseparably married to love; good tidings spoken harshly are not good tidings. The charm of the message is destroyed by the difficult spirit or even attitude of the messenger.

Then as the four leadership gifts (the offices we reviewed) equip the saints, and as the saints become active in service, they [5] **grow up in every way and in all things into Him Who is the Head.**

Every area of life—more and more—become increasingly *like Him.* Members of His body are to be evidence of "Christ-likeness."

> Next, the wonderful 16th verse. **For because of Him the whole body (the church, in all its various parts), closely joined and firmly knit together by the joints and ligaments with which it is supplied, when each part [with power adapted to its need] is working properly [in all its functions], grows to full maturity, building itself up in love.**

Growth comes from Jesus. From Him **the whole body** is involved in this "growth." All **closely joined and firmly knit.**

Every member designed for his own place and joined with every other!

The human body consists primarily of bones, organs and flesh. I recommend you read "The Case For A Creator."[27]

> Joints and ligaments bind our bones. Ligaments attach our organs. Each joint, each ligament fulfills a role in growth. To go further, the body is made up of millions of cells, each designed for its own purpose, all working together to benefit the body. From Strobel's book: "The entire cell can be viewed

as a factory that contains an elaborate network of interlocking assembly lines, each of which is composed of a set of large protein machines. These protein assemblies contain highly coordinated moving parts."

So it is in the Body of Christ! Each believer is a cell in the body—each cell contributing to the whole, each one finding its proper location. Amazing isn't it?

At the end of v. 16, we read ***building itself up in love***. Love is the circulatory system of the body. Isolate a baby, he will not grow properly, and will be more susceptible to disease. Do not be an isolated Christian; you will never minister to others in the body, ***building itself up in love.*** Love unites, selfishness divides.

As each member ministers his proper role, "the body" grows as a single harmonious unit. Not only in size but also building itself up in love. This is what the entire world really wants, a concern for one another in the body.

Section Five
Additional Questions and Thoughts for Discussion

1. Discuss the difference between Position and Practice.
2. How does a believer 'walk worthy' of being *in Christ?*
3. What does the life style of a believer consist of?
4. What is the basis for unity among believers?
5. How does patience aid in unity?
6. How does Paul explain unity?
7. What place does disunity have in the Church?
8. Why did the author conclude there are four leadership offices?
9. Be honest! Are leaders equipping you for ministry?

THIRTEEN

Remove the Dirty Clothes

W e continue with the second area of **THE PRACTICE OF THE BELIEVER** (refer to Outline in cp. ONE). We looked at **Body Parts,** now this section is **Morality** of these parts. We will review this section in three paragraphs. The first is verses 17-24.

This begins Paul's appeal for a new morality. He seems to reach out and call for a new era, a change in society because life is now *in Christ* (that wonderful theme from Ephesians cp. 1). This is Paul's call for a social change. The thoughts in these verses carry through to the end of Ephesians.

The very fact that we are now *in Christ*, ought to motivate us to walk in purity. Similar to Paul's words to the Romans in 6:4 *so we too might [habitually] live and behave in newness of life*.

We are now alive in Christ, not dead in sins.

> Take off the **old dirty death-clothes** and put on the **new clean grace-clothes**!
>
> ¹⁷ *So this I say and solemnly testify in [the name of] the Lord*

We see Paul is writing *in the name of the Lord* or by authority of the Lord. It is by this divine authority that he urges Christians to put off every trace of their past life, to take off the clothes worn during spiritual death, *then*, put on the Excellencies of Jesus.

There *are* negatives in our walk, and here is one. He says **that you must no longer**—Or, you are no longer Gentiles! You are Christians. Your life should change by walking away from what is happening in a Christ-less world. Christians are not to imitate the life of unsaved people surrounding them. Turn away *from* and turn *towards*. In fact, in Ephesians cp. 5 Paul will say we should **imitate God**.

A WORLD WITHOUT CHRIST

Terrible things characterize the world without Christ. Paul will remind his readers of some very important truths taking place in the world. In looking at this, we see *seven characteristics*, which progress from one to another. Notice the progression. This further amplifies what Paul has said earlier. This is additional explanation about being dead (which we reviewed). Now we say *take off the dirty clothes of death*. Let me summarize these seven characteristic of our world without Christ:

> We will name #1 **Empty** from the latter part of [17] **as the heathen (the Gentiles) do in their perverseness [in the folly, vanity, and emptiness of their souls and the futility] of their minds.**

Their life was empty. PUT THIS OFF. There was a lot of activity, but no progress in God. They chased after "bubbles" and neglected the realities of life. This could be a picture of today's generation.

> #2 we will name **Dark 18a** *Their moral understanding is darkened and their reasoning is clouded.*

They suffered darkness or blindness because of a rejection of the trueness of God. "Rejection of truth = Blindness"

We could also say they had a dark mind; we have these words "***understanding***" and "***reasoning***" (which was dark). Light was available, but darkness was all they accepted. It was almost as though darkness was the only thing they craved. Paul is saying: PUT THIS OFF.

> #3 is **Hardness 18b** *[They are] alienated (estranged, self-banished) from the life of God [with no share in it; this is] because of the ignorance (the want of knowledge and perception, the willful blindness) that is <u>deep-seated</u> in them, due to their hardness of heart.* (Underline added for emphasis)

Notice the emptiness and wandering mind that leads to darkness of God's Truth, which now leads to a hardened heart.

The Greek word for "hardness" means "stone." Usually referring to an extremely hard marble—even petrified. Sometimes this same word was used as a medical term: A stiffening of joints, arthritis, or hardening of bones.

The world without Christ, which he describes, is alienated and is a great distance from God. They plunged into idolatry and wandered further and further from God. *Remember* these are seven characteristics *of a world without Christ!* We must remind ourselves of these, put them off, and keep them off.

Of course, this is a picture of *any* society, *any* time in history—including today!

Then we see that a dark mind, which became aimless then blind, and led to a hardened heart, now produces a sin-filled shameless life:

> #4 is in 19 *In their spiritual apathy they have become callous and past feeling and reckless and have abandoned themselves [a prey] to unbridled sensuality . . .*

Shameless

They got over any pain of separation. They silenced the voice of God in their heart; in spiritual apathy, they became callous. The twinge of abandoning God was less acute. PUT THIS OFF!

This is a shameful place to have fallen. A terrible place to be. How sad! Steady rejection—results in separation, *lost.* We reviewed this "place" in an earlier lesson, explaining that it is possible that God stops loving a person. It would be good to understand that earlier illustration of being in light, and *willingly* walking to the depths of a dark cave.

The next three characteristics are also found in v. 19.

We will name #5 **Impure.**

Impure is a state described as "dark and dirty, depressingly wretched, and intentionally selfish." That best describes this next step of the unbeliever.

> Verse 19 continues *. . . . eager and greedy to indulge in every form of impurity*

Vile forms of behavior including sexual impurity.

> The next one #6, **Indecent.** *eager and greedy to indulge in every form of impurity.* They seem to give themselves up to every kind of "uncleanness" as if it were their very business in life.

> #7, **Unsatisfied.** *eager and greedy to indulge in every form of impurity[that their depraved desires may suggest and demand].*

Imagine the picture: Never satisfied, never enough. They had an appetite for more and more ungodliness. Paul paints that picture of a world without Christ.

However, thanks to God, he goes on—another of those great transformational thoughts. You may remember ***"But God"*** in 2:4 and ***"but now in Christ"*** in 2:13; we have a similar transition in [20] ***But you did not so learn Christ!*** Put off the dirty clothes of spiritual death!

How different these seven characteristics were from ***Christ*** who the Ephesians had come to know and love! They had learned Christ! They put off the seven characteristics of the one outside of Christ. No longer did these worldly characteristics exist in them. They now had come alive, *in Christ*. They learned Christ! The dirty clothes exchanged for grace clothes.

Jesus knew *no* sin

Jesus did *no* sin

There was *no sin* in Jesus. They had learned Christ. Paul was saying, "You did not so learn these things from Christ" or *in Christ*.

Verse 21 is emphasizing the true conversion that they experienced. Notice Paul did not say, "You didn't learn *about* Christ." They heard of Him, and perhaps studied Him. A person can learn *about* Him and never *learn* Him. Are you with me? I can learn *about* a great scholar, maybe Tozar or Wigglesworth, but never *learn them*—they are both dead. Jesus is alive so I can learn *Him* through a personal fellowship *with* Him.

Paul goes on: ²¹ Assuming *that you have really heard Him and been taught by Him, as [all] Truth is in Jesus [embodied and personified in Him],*

The Ephesus believers had *heard Him* with the hearing of faith. Many hear—but do not really receive or understand. Are you still with me?

He had taught these believers. They came to know His holiness and godliness.

Read these wonderful words of John in 1 John 1:1 *Whom we have heard, Whom we have seen with our [own] eyes, Whom we have gazed upon [for ourselves] and have touched with our [own] hands.* We looked at Him, we touched Him, and we really heard Him.

The hearing was the truth (v. 21) *as [all] Truth is in Jesus.* John 14:6 says *He is truth incarnate.*

Paul refers back to the walk on earth as a man (referred to by calling His name Jesus). He says Jesus walked with a spotless life, the very antithesis of the walk of Gentiles, which Paul just described in those seven characteristics.

> Paul refers again in v. 22 to their *former nature; your old unrenewed self he* says. *Strip yourselves of your former nature [put off and discard your old unrenewed self] which characterized your previous manner of life and becomes corrupt through lusts and desires that spring from delusion*.

This is referring to the person, and who he was as a child of Adam, before he became one of the adopted sons of God. This was the *old man*. We *were* children of the first man, Adam but *now* believers are children of the last Adam, Jesus Christ.

The old life was corrupt, resulting from giving in to deceitful cravings, the seven progressions we previously reviewed.

Paul emphasizes the *new* position of a believer: He is a new man of grace who put off the old man!

A simple illustration of this great truth is given in John's Gospel, the resurrection of Lazarus. Lazarus had been in the grave four days. The body was decaying. Notice our Lord's words: *Free him of the burial wrappings and let him go*. (John 11:44). Take off the death clothes! Lazarus no longer belonged to the old dominion of death, for he was now alive. Why go about wearing death clothes? Take off the old and put on the new! That is what Jesus said and what Paul is telling his readers.

Verse 23 continues Paul's picture. The Ephesus believers were being renewed. **ASK:** *How do we take off the dirty clothes of spiritual death?*

> ²³*And be constantly renewed in the spirit of your mind [having a fresh mental and spiritual attitude],*

A complete about-face in thinking is needed. As the mind understands the truth of God's Word, it is gradually transformed and renewed by the Holy Spirit and leads to a changed life. *As he thinks in his heart so is he.* (Proverbs 23:7)

*²⁴ **And put on the new nature (the regenerate self) created in God's image, [Godlike] in true righteousness and holiness.***

The Ephesus believers had put on a new nature. This *new man* contrasts with the *old man*; the seven characteristics that *we* shouted out PUT THIS OFF, and have removed.

He is reminding them again how a believer **in Christ** is new. He is a new creation, old things have passed away and all things have become new. Created to be like God in nature, it manifests **in true righteousness and holiness.**

FOURTEEN

Put On New, Clean Clothes

We continue in Ephesians 4 with vv. 25-32. You remember, Paul gave seven characteristics of a world without Christ—and reminded us to avoid a progression into decay and death to which they lead.

Paul then moves on to what this *new man* should demonstrate in his life. **ASK:** *How are Christians to be in this world?*

Remember, Paul is looking at the **Practice of the Believer**. What should *the new* man put on? He talked about the old man and seven characteristics to *put off*. Paul never moves on until he has explained a principle. Paul calls sin, sin, and then makes sure he calls it sin! He mentions *five different sins* in this section that believers should be aware of and avoid. We should be *dead* to these. The first of the new clothes to put on is concerning telling the truth and controlling anger. We must keep in mind in this continued topic: You and I do not *put off and then put on clothing as if reaching in a closet,* and lifting the change of clothes from a hanger! Spiritually, only Christ removes the old clothing and dresses one in the new clothing. He is the only One who has that ability.

> [25] *Therefore, rejecting all falsity and being done now with it, let everyone express the truth with his neighbor, for we are all parts of one body and members one of another.* Earlier Paul said *lovingly express truth*

#1: LYING "*rejecting all falsity,*" or reject all lying. The believer is to *avoid* all lying and must speak the truth.

Paul is directly referring to the Christian believers in Ephesus. At one time, they embraced a lie of false gods. Now they have turned to the truth of One God.

This word lying includes every form of dishonesty. There are no "white lies"; every lie causes injury to someone.

- Shading of truth
- Exaggeration
- Cheating
- Failure to keep promises
- Flattery
- Fudging on income taxes

A lie is a "fact spoken with the intent to deceive." If I tell you it is 12 o'clock noon and make a mistake because I did not change my watch, it is not a lie. However, if I tell you the wrong time in order to make you miss a meeting, it is a lie. The very word "false" includes an intentional deception.

#2: ANGER, [26] *When angry, do not sin; do not ever let your wrath (your exasperation, your fury or indignation) last until the sun goes down.* (Good advice, why not use the sun going down, as a check point). [27] *Leave no [such] room or foothold for the devil [give no opportunity to him].* (Comment in parenthesis added by author)

Anger is an emotion—caused by something that upsets or displeases. It is trying to control the situation that is not going your way. It is the opposite of love. It may "set you off." In itself, anger for the right reason, is not a sin. Read about God's anger. Deuteronomy 9:8 reads, *"He was angry."* Jeremiah 4:8 says *"the fierce anger of the Lord."* Moreover, He never sinned. His anger is a part of His judgment against sin. Why would you believe God would ignore sin and leave it unjudged?

There are times when a believer may be righteously angry.

Certainly when *God's character* is slandered, anger is commanded. Anger against evil can be righteous.

We *should* express some anger with sin. However, when anger is associated with resentment, jealousy, or hatred, it is forbidden. It is against the new man's nature.

Jesus was angry and cleansed the temple in Matthew 21:12. He also said it's the first step toward murder in Matthew 5; and he said if you do slip into anger, "go to that one and talk it out" (Matthew 5:25 and 18:15). That takes a man! Rather, that takes a believer.

Anyone can become angry; that is easy. We are emotional people. However, to be angry with the right person, to the right degree, at the right time, for the right purpose, and in the right way . . . . *that* . . . . is not easy!

If a believer gives in to unrighteous wrath, confess it! Do not ignore the emotion; do not let it pass without addressing it. Paul tells us to [26] **not ever let your wrath (your exasperation, your fury or indignation) last until the sun goes down.**

Giving in to wrath *permits a place* for the devil to work, and we don't need to assist in giving him a place in our lives. He attempts that in many ways on his own.

Notice [27] **Leave no [such] room or foothold for the devil [give no opportunity to him].** The words used here, **room or foothold,** in the Greek (*topos*) refers to a specific marked off location. The devil is out to take all or any territory of your life. That region of your life could be *health, wealth, employment, emotions, relationships, marriage,* etc. Any *room* has a door he tries to enter. So close every opening in your life. I allow him no entry point, and tell him to stay out in his world.

> Then #3 of these five sins to avoid: **STEALING.** Paul turns to contrasting *stealing* and *sharing.* [28] **Let the thief steal no more, but rather let him be industrious, making an honest living with his own hands, so that he may be able to give to those in need.** We recognize here the eighth commandment. I would note that every one of these five topics is linked to the Ten Commandments in some way.

The *old* man *steals*, the *new* man always *shares*.

Paul may have known that some of his readers were thieves. It seems some were stealing to give to others in order to reap the benefits from Christ; Acts 20:35 *does* inform us **It is more blessed (makes one happier and more to be envied) to give than to receive.**

Paul addresses Christians. Christians apparently are not perfect. They still have some of that *old nature* in them they must deal with, perhaps every day. Some of the old clothes are still being worn.

Stealing may take many forms (similar to lying, which we discussed):

From grand larceny to non-payment of debts

Perhaps wasting an employer's time

From shop lifting to taking an employer's supplies

False expense accounts including travel summaries

We steal many other ways. We can steal time from being with God in worship. I can see how we steal from God by not finding our *gift (s)* and using them. We can steal by not using time wisely in our place of employment or overcharging for a product we sell. Stealing has many forms.

Only the power of grace can turn a thief into a giver.

A spirit of giving is a wonderful thing. Years ago when I met a Christian who had a spirit of greed, I made a decision in my life, to receive by faith, a spirit of giving. Let us be givers.

Always know that Satan is not "only" a liar and a murderer, he also is a thief—that great verse of John 10:10 **steal and kill and destroy.** Satan turned Judas into a thief (John 12:6), and he would do the same to us if he could. When he tempted Eve, he led her to become a thief; she took what she was not supposed to have. In addition, Adam became a thief. So as a result, God removed both of them from the garden. The first Adam was a thief; the last Adam turned to a thief and said He would be with Him in paradise.

Then Paul turns to the *speech* of a believer in v. 29:

#4: CORRUPT SPEECH, [29] *Let no foul or polluting language, nor evil word nor unwholesome or worthless talk [ever] come out of your mouth, but only such [speech] as is good and beneficial to the spiritual progress of others, as is fitting to the need and the occasion, that it may be a blessing and give grace (God's favor) to those who hear it.*

He contrasts that which is *worthless* to that which *edifies*.

Let no foul or polluting language, nor evil word nor unwholesome or worthless talk [ever] come out of your mouth,

WOW! *That* is to be your conversation. Words are powerful. Do not ever let your conversation suggest filthiness in any way. Never cut another person down with your words:

Off-color jokes

Dirty stories to add to the office conversation

Any kind of profanity. Not even a little shade of darkness, so as not to come across too "square." Everybody does it—don't they?

Criticism

Paul is saying—just *don't!*

The word **unwholesome** is quite clear in the Greek. It was used to describe rotten fruit. It can be translated "putrid" or "corrupt." Enough said!

Paul will deal with foul language early in Ephesians cp. 5. Here he is telling us to abandon *profitless speech* and substitute meaningful and constructive conversation. It seems to deal with any form of conversation that is empty or worthless. That is not easy, it takes discipline.

He says *our* conversation should be:

#1 Uplifting; build whomever you talk with. It is a ministry of every believer. Say things that will encourage others to keep on. Stay away from the negatives in your conversations.

#2 Proper; suitable to the occasion in which we are involved.

#3 Gracious; it should impart grace to the hearer. Let's impart grace in every conversation. *Practice this for the next twenty-four hours.*

Examine these three—use them as a guideline in your conversations. If your words are not uplifting, proper and gracious—*don't.*

Then, keeping in context, if v. 30 is connected to v. 29, our worthless talk grieves the Holy Spirit, [30]***And do not grieve the Holy Spirit of God [do not offend or sadden Him], by Whom you were sealed (marked, branded as God's own, secured) for the day of redemption***

In addition, if linked to this whole paragraph, which I believe it is, then unrighteous anger, lying and stealing *also* hurt Him. Just makes sense doesn't it? The Holy Spirit, a Person, is living in the temple of each believer. We do not want to offend Him.

Let me suggest three connected reasons, which are given for this hurt:

He is . . . . *The **Holy** Spirit.* Anything that is not holy is distasteful to Him.

He is . . . . *The Holy Spirit **of God.*** Always acknowledge Him as an equal member of the Trinity of God.

In addition, we ***were sealed*** by Him, for the great final day of redemption.

The very fact that the Holy Spirit can be grieved shows indeed He is a Person. It says that *He loves us*, for only a person who loves can be *grieved.*

In v. 31, we will see that all sins of temper and tongue should be put away.

Verse 30 reads ***And grieve not the Holy Spirit of God, whereby ye are sealed unto the day of redemption.***

The Greek word for ***grieve*** is *lupete*. Quite simple it means *a grief that can only be experienced by people who love one another*. Since *lupete* would generally refer to the result of one married party being unfaithful to the other, Paul's use of the word in *reference to the Holy Spirit* is quite unusual. As a result of the unfaithfulness, the betrayed one is grieved because of the pain caused.

We learn here that a believer and the Holy Spirit have a close, tender relationship. The Holy Spirit loves us, desires to talk with us, and share our feelings and goals.

When we *lupete* by putting on dirty clothes of "acting like the world" or responding in a way the world responds, *we hurt the Spirit inside us.* We actually take Him with us into the world we are acting like! Think about the Holy Spirit: He drew us to God, placed us in Christ, worked to mature us, and empowered us. When we sin, we grieve Him. Would we dare to walk Him into darkness?

One unknown scholar has translated Ephesians 4:30 in the following way:

"Stop deeply wounding and causing such extreme emotional pain to the Spirit of God, by whom you have been sealed until the day of your redemption."

Oh! I plead with you to realize how precious He is. Ask Him to respond to you by telling you any hurt that you have caused Him. Then make it right.

> **#5** in this list of sins to be done away with, **BITTERNESS,**
> [31] ***Let all bitterness and indignation and wrath (passion, rage, bad temper) and resentment (anger, animosity) and quarreling (brawling, clamor, contention) and slander (evil-speaking, abusive or blasphemous language) be banished from you, with all malice (spite, ill will, or baseness of any kind).***

Paul, being the scholar that he was, generally used many words to amplify the doctrine at hand. He named several kinds of anger. He is saying remove every trace of anger quickly. Do not let it even begin, because it leads to bondage.

We find in this verse:

A smoldering resentment, unwillingness to forgive. **Wrath**; outbursts of **temper.**

We read here, **anger** again—grouchiness, hostility. This is an attitude of hatred.

We could call it clamor; loud outcries of anger, **brawling**, bickering, shouting down of opponents.

Evil-speaking is listed; insulting language, slander about another, gossiping.

In addition, **malice**—wishing evil on another. Deliberately trying to harm people.

Only a believer yielded to Christ and the Holy Spirit in sincerity and full dedication will experience the solution for the tongue being tamed. It cannot be done by the mere work of flesh and mind.

Paul follows those hurtful attitudes with the *attitudes that replace them*, in v. 32. **And become useful and helpful and kind to one another, tenderhearted (compassionate, understanding, loving-hearted), forgiving one another [readily and freely], as God in Christ forgave you.**

Here we find *kindness (an opposite of bitterness/malice)*—an unselfish concern for the welfare of others, and a desire to be helpful even at great personal sacrifice.

We find *tenderheartedness (not wrath/or angry)*—A sympathetic, affectionate, and compassionate interest in others, and a willingness to bear their burden.

Paul makes the final demand for new attitudes: *forgiveness (not resentment or unwillingness to forgive);* this is being in readiness to pardon offenses, to overlook personal wrongs against oneself, and to harbor no desire for retaliation.

The greatest example of One who forgives—is God Himself, which returns to Paul's ongoing theme: **In Christ**, that is, in His Person and work, God found the righteous basis on which He could forgive us. Moreover, since he forgave us when we were "millions of dollars" in debt, so should we forgive the one who owes us a few dollars.

At *the very time* someone wrongs *me*, I must forgive him! Hard to do? Yes. It is hard to imagine or accept as being mandatory. Putting off the anger and the need to strike back or return the hurt is a relief! It is freedom.

Forgiveness is actually for our benefit. Releasing our anger and the need to return hurt will free us from frustration. Always forgive in the way you want to be forgiven. *The person's response is not your concern.* Whether he/she asks my pardon makes no difference. The importance is in the fact that I have instantly forgiven him. He must face God with the wrong he has done; but that is his and God's affair.

FIFTEEN

Imitate God

We continue in this Section **THE MORALITY OF BELIEVERS** with the second paragraph, Ephesians 5:1-20. Paul again emphasizes the new believer in contrast to the spiritually dead person.

Paul extends his teaching here, from the example of God's forgiveness he used in v. 32 of cp. 4, where he said *forgiving one another [readily and freely], as God in Christ forgave you.* He had mentioned five sins that believers are to avoid and then gave a replacement for each one.

This is the "connection" continuing into cp. 5: God in Christ has forgiven you [1] *THEREFORE BE imitators of God* in forgiving one another. Copy God, follow His example. This statement is startling! Nowhere else in the Bible is such an admonition declared. How could there be any higher standard set? We could determine to be like any other person in history—but imitate God? Yet Paul directs us to act like the Supreme Ruler of the universe!

How is this possible? Think of who God is. We many times consider His attributes in order to know Him.

- He has no beginning or end
- He needs no help to accomplish the task
- He is in all places at the same time
- He is all-powerful
- He knows everything

- Moreover, add to this, His glory

We do not, nor will we ever have these attributes.

Paul says first, we are to imitate God **as well-beloved children.** In setting the theme for this area in Ephesians, Paul is saying, it is natural to see children imitate their parents. That can be both encouraging and embarrassing.

When my daughter was a small girl, she wanted to be like her mom. I remember when her mom slipped on a curb and sprained her foot. The next day I noticed she came from a room with a noticeable "limp." Right behind her was our daughter—you guessed it—showing an exaggerated "limp." She just wanted to be like mom, to imitate her.

Paul uses this word "imitators" several times in his writings. It is the Greek word *mimetes*, which means to act like what you see someone else doing. People who acted on the stage for their profession were said to *mimetes.* It also depicted the modeling of a parent, teacher, champion, or hero.

Paul used the word *mimetes* when he told the Corinthians **So I urge and implore you, be imitators of me** (1 Corinthians 4:16). Using the Greek meaning, this verse could be translated, *"I'm urging you to act like me! Watch what I do, and duplicate in your own life everything you see in me."*

In Second Thessalonians 3:7, Paul again used the word *mimetes* when he told the Thessalonians **For you yourselves know how it is necessary to imitate our example.** This verse could be translated, *"It is quite important for you to follow our example, follow us and duplicate the things you notice in our lives."*

Mimetes is found in Hebrews 6:12 **In order that you may not grow disinterested and become [spiritual] sluggards, but <u>imitators,</u> behaving as do those who through faith (by their leaning of the entire personality on God in Christ in absolute trust and confidence in His power, wisdom, and goodness) and by practice of patient endurance and waiting are [now] inheriting the promises.** (Underline added for emphasis)

Then Hebrews 13:7 also uses the word *mimetes.* **Remember your leaders and superiors in authority [for it was they] who brought to you** *the Word of God. Observe attentively and consider their manner of living (the outcome of their well-spent lives) and imitate their faith.*

The last section of that verse could be translated, *"You should model your faith after theirs; act like them, say what they are saying, considering the fruit produce by their lives."*

From these verses, we understand what Paul is telling us. We must model our lives after God. An actor attempts to capture the emotions, looks, voice, character, and even the appearance of the person he is portraying. Therefore, we are to put our whole heart and soul into imitating God in every sphere of our lives. This means we must make a decision *to act like God*!

We also note how Paul began v. 1. It opens with **THEREFORE BE.** The Greek word used here is the word *ginomai*; however, here it appears slightly different and would be better translated: *"Always be in the process of becoming."* It is the idea of a person starting some specific action and is now continuing to work on it. The goal has yet to be met—but he is committed to keep working on it and remaining in the process. We say, "Keep on keeping on."

There are times when we *disguise* an inner feeling by "acting." Each one of us has that ability. Each one of us can act. This is what Paul is saying. You may have certain offended feelings at times but are still required to act *like Him*. No, of course you should never think you are God, but we *are told* to act like Him. Moreover, note that acting-like-God is not something you will attain the first time tried. To capture His character, you will have to spend time in prayer and be committed. *Trust the Holy Spirit* who is in you. He will help establish and direct you. Make a conscientious decision to act like Him today, then perhaps tomorrow increasing your actions. Keep acting like God in your daily activities until you finally begin to think like God, talk like God, sound like God, and carry yourself in the confidence of God!

As we consider the continued thoughts of v. 1, we could paraphrase this first thought as *"At all times be in the process of becoming more like God; actually acting like Him and duplicating Him in every area of your life."*

A LOVE WALK

Verse 2 suggests *how* to imitate God, **And walk in love**; the remainder of the verse explains that walking in love means to reach out and give ourselves for others.

Christ is our example of love. His life, His act of giving, is what proved His love. This verse ties back to the last two verses of cp. 4.

I like how Paul explains it. Christ was an offering, and **sacrifice to God**. An offering is anything given to God while a **sacrifice** includes the element of death.

Jesus was the One who was completely dedicated to do the will of God, even to the death on a cross. *That is love.* This sacrifice became [2] **a sweet fragrance,** a wonderful aroma to God. It was a sweet fragrance around the throne of God. When God sees one of His children doing acts of His love, a fragrance encircles the throne.

Paul gives his reason why every believer is to walk in love. There is some repetition of his previous comments in his saying [3b] **as is fitting and proper among saints.** He lists these dark patches or groupings of immoral sins while forcefully calling for a separation *from* them.

> [3] **But immorality (sexual vice) and all impurity [of lustful, rich, wasteful living] or greediness must not even be named among you, as is fitting and proper among saints (God's consecrated people).**
> [4] **Let there be no filthiness (obscenity, indecency) nor foolish and sinful (silly and corrupt) talk, nor coarse jesting, which are not fitting or becoming; but instead voice your thankfulness [to God].**

This list of wrong doings (sins) is part of the darkness and has no place in the new life. The two are opposite societies.

Paul includes some specific forms of sexual wrongs that **must not even be named among you.** They speak for themselves. Because a change has taken place in his readers, Paul makes it clear their life is the opposite of these "wrong doings." God has made the Church spiritually alive as opposed to the spiritually dead. Believers are lights shining in the world of darkness.

We see *immorality* in v. 3, which refers to any kind of illicit sexual wrongdoing. Our English word pornography has its roots here. You recognize this quickly from the Greek word "*porneia*." Paul will discuss the believer's response to this later in the chapter.

The words *impurity and filthiness* are used to amplify this topic; probably related to impure pictures, obscene books and just about anything that feeds the fires of passion.

In addition, *greediness* is here, not for money, as we would normally think of this word, but rather a greediness to satisfy a sexual need outside of marriage.

These things *must not even be named among you*. Do not even discuss them as to make an excuse for this type of sin—perhaps even taking them lightly.

Paul adds here a comment, with this phrase: As *is fitting and proper among saints.* He again refers to *saints*; thank God that these dark sins are no longer in your life. All these negative characteristics and traits that we see here—and more which he lists can be overcome, in Christ. He says [4b] *But instead.* Also, remember, instead of feeling hopeless about your failures, go to God and ask Him to forgive you. His blood was shed for everyone, which would include these dark sins. Nothing you have done is too big for his blood. He wants to forgive and cleanse you even more than you want to confess.

Paul adds in v. 4 that their speech is now free from some things; (similar to what we learned from vv. 25-29 of cp. 4). The many sins of the tongue are really sins of the heart. It is easy to see the connection between vv. 3 and 4. That appetite of impurity leads to a speech problem. [4] *Let there be no filthiness (obscenity, indecency) nor foolish and sinful (silly and corrupt) talk, nor coarse jesting, which are not fitting or becoming.*

We reviewed some of this subject in Paul's treatment of the sins *to be put off*, in Chapter FOURTEEN of this course.

Now Paul adds unclean stories, suggestive jokes, and indecency. They are no longer a part of the believer's actions. This *coarse jesting* is a word that means "able to turn easily" or turning any conversation into an 'out of place' comment. This *foolish and silly talk* is not innocent—it is senseless conversation that cheapens the man. It is not fitting, not accomplishing a good purpose. Paul is not referring to good humor when he uses *foolish.*

We know the Bible says we should be happy, joyful, and have a merry heart. Clean jokes, riddles, and fun stories lift people's hearts. *A happy heart is good medicine and a cheerful mind works healing,* Proverbs 17:22. He is not referring to good fruit. The entire context deals with impurity. He is talking about impure or even selfish conversation that destroys reputations and tears down other people's self-image.

You can understand what he is saying as he concludes his thoughts: Put away the foolish talking and jesting, [4b] *but instead voice your thankfulness [to God].*

Thankfulness for what? Be thankful for all the characteristics of God that flow into the person *in Christ*; all the character of Christ is now inside you. Life, health, blessings—all His fullness were born in you. We might think back at all the vices mentioned, and be thankful for what I call "the blessing from the other side."

Each one of the topics Paul listed can be thought about from the opposite meaning. The *opposite* of immoral sex is God's view of marital sex. It has been given by God, is itself good, and is therefore something for which we should be thankful. The *opposite* side of greed is giving—again for which we should thankful. Be thankful for the material gains in life. Jesting and silly talk—has an *opposite* to be used—build up and encourage others in the goodness of God. Just think of giving thanks to God for all things.

> And to leave no doubt as to God's attitude he's very clear: [5]
> *For be sure of this: that no person practicing sexual vice or impurity in thought or in life, or one who is covetous has any inheritance in the kingdom of Christ and of God.*
> Perfectly clear.

Today's society many times calls it *sickness*—God calls it *sin*

Men condone it—God condemns it. *Men say the answer is psychoanalysis, God says the answer is regeneration.*

Notice the deity of Christ comes forth in these words [5] *the kingdom of Christ and of God.* Christ is placed on equal level with God the Father as Ruler in the kingdom. Again this emphasizes believers are saints and members of His kingdom.

Then an additional comment [6] ***Let no one delude and deceive you***. This is the second reminder by Paul not to be fooled. Do not just go along with the world's thinking on these areas.

I encourage each believer to walk in the character of Christ in all things. You can just walk away from the office stories. You can look the other way. [7] ***So do not associate or be sharers with them.***

SIXTEEN

Light and Darkness

P aul next reemphasizes a previous theme—A few thoughts on darkness and light in vv. 8-14. As *saints*, we walk as light.

He repeats how the readers were once *darkness*, notice: [8] **For once you were darkness . . . but now you are light in the Lord.** Precisely stated. At one time, the Ephesus believers *were* darkness, now they *are* light.

Think about the metaphor Paul uses here. Spiritually, each of us walks in darkness until we receive the light of Christ in our lives. At one time, we were unsure about God, or unsure we were pleasing Him. Problems would throw us into confusion, and at times, we felt hopeless, trying to make ourselves into something good. Then we surrendered to God and light came in. What a difference! It was like walking into a dark room, stumbling around, fumbling for a switch on the wall to turn on the light. Immediately light came and darkness was dispelled. With light, we now have the wisdom to work out the problems and actually know the Father accepts us.

Notice Paul did not say they were *in* darkness; they *were* darkness. Now through union with Christ they have become light! Not just walking in light! Read it again: [8] **For once you were darkness . . . but now you are light in the Lord.** Paul personifies Dark and Light.

This is a picture of each of us! We *are*—light of the world, we do not just *live in* light. Moreover, as light, we should walk as light 24/7. This is Paul's main thrust of the passage.

> In v. 9 Paul lists three main words that are the type of fruit that characterize a life walking as light. [9] *For the fruit (the effect, the product) of the Light or the Spirit [consists] in every form of kindly goodness, uprightness of heart, and trueness of life.*

The fruit of the Spirit consists of all forms of goodness, righteousness and truth. Light produces or matures the fruit.

> ***Goodness:*** A term for all moral excellence. It is the ability to respond to other people with right motives and love.

> ***Uprightness:*** This is righteousness and means integrity in all dealings with God and men. It is the knowledge of the right way to behave because in Gods sight we have already been made His righteousness.

> ***Trueness of life:*** The knowing and expressing God's perspective on every action of life. This is ***trueness of*** your very ***life.*** Examine the truth of your life. The light produces this fruit as surely as the sun light develops apples and bananas! Develop and grow the fruit.

Joining these three, you have the light of a Christ-filled life, shining into darkness. Paul says [10] ***try to learn what is pleasing to the Lord.***

Put every area of life under the searchlight.

We were in a service in Kansas City a few years ago when the pastor told us: "Every time I leave church after preaching, as I approach my car, I ask God, 'Was my attitude, my words, my actions, right in your site?'"

Examine your life in Christ: The books you read, clothes you wear, friendships, vacations, entertainments, everything! **ASK:** *How do these activities of life affect light to others?*

Believers should ¹¹***Take no part in and have no fellowship with the fruitless deeds and enterprises of darkness, but instead expose and reprove and convict them.***

We are clearly told not to be a part of any form of darkness. Don't even tolerate it. If light does not shine, the shadow of darkness appears.

Works of darkness are unfruitful as far as God is concerned. These works of darkness are nothing but locked, dim rooms that light must *flood into* and *expose.*

A life of holiness and words of correction (always under the careful direction of the Holy Spirit), will shine into darkness. Light always scatters darkness.

> Verse 12 serves as a caution. It explains why the Christian should have no connection with secret, dark sins and why he should rebuke those sins. ¹²***For it is a shame even to speak of or mention the things that [such people] practice in secret.***

Do not even talk about such sins, for just the mentioning or describing them may defile the minds of the listeners! However, your light will manifest whatever is in the darkness. Think of that!

> ¹³***But when anything is exposed and reproved by the light, it is made visible and clear.***

Jesus ***reproved*** the hypocrisy of the Pharisees and exposed it even though the disciples did not understand or realize the evilness of hypocrisy. All Jesus had to do, as Light, was to be in the presence of Pharisees and their true character was revealed. Light ***exposed*** dark.

The latter part of v. 13 could read *and where everything is (MADE) visible and clear there is light.*

This means that when Christians exercise their *ministry as light,* others are brought *to the light.* I believe that *many* who live in darkness are transformed through your ministry of light! A few may not because of their will. Your life as a believer and your part in His Kingdom is to let light shine! That is your part in His Kingdom.

[14] Therefore He says, Awake, O sleeper, and arise from the dead, and Christ shall shine upon you and give you light.

Your life should always expose any surrounding darkness. It should always preach a sermon. This verse is the voice of light, speaking to those sleeping in darkness. *Awake, O sleeper.* We belong to light. Jesus *shouted with a loud voice,* in John 11:43 *Lazarus, come out!* And light came out of the dark!

A CONTRAST

In the next seven verses, Paul contrasts various foolish footsteps with a proper conduct. He uses a series of negative and positive exhortations.

He starts with a general overall plea: *[15] Look carefully then how you walk!*

You may recall we listed at the beginning of this course several key words. *Walk* is one of those key words in Ephesians.

It is mentioned seven times (2:10; 4:1, 17; 5:2, 8, 15) to fully describe the entire life of an individual. This is his/her "walk." Verse 15 continues *Live purposefully and worthily and accurately, not as the unwise and witless, but as wise.*

Do not walk as unwise and fools do! Absolutely clear. We are to walk in His wisdom. The Greek carries the idea of accuracy. We could understand this as "See that you walk carefully, with exactness." Only a fool drifts along with the wind—the believer marks out his course, sets his sails, guides the rudder. Evil is all around us. Christians need to be wise and live pleasing to the Lord. Seek Him for every step you take. The Holy Spirit resides in you to assist you. Trust Him. The first third of the Book of Proverbs pictures God's Wisdom standing in the streets, crying out for the believer to pursue her. Paul in 1 Corinthians 1:23-24 speaks out against the foolish wisdom of the Greeks and contrasts it with *We preach Christ (the Messiah) crucified, [preaching which] to the Jews is a scandal and an offensive stumbling block [that springs a snare or trap], and to the Gentiles it is absurd and utterly unphilosophical nonsense. [24] But to*

those who are called, whether Jew or Greek (Gentile), Christ [is] the Power of God and the Wisdom of God.

Continuing in this Ephesians passage, [16] ***Making the very most of the time, because the days are evil.***

The walk of wisdom calls us to redeem the time, or "buy every opportunity." Time indeed is short. Each new day brings open doors for acts of mercy and words of help. Make the most of every day! I like to *purposefully choose* to do some act of kindness each day and watch for the opportunity to redeem a special moment.

Each day also presents the evil character that exists, ***the days are evil.*** Perhaps you have noticed this! In Paul's time, this meant that Roman persecution was on the way. This is perhaps what Paul was considering. Win the lost while there is time—do good while there is time to affect another's life. Each of us must walk strongly in Christ. Today may be the last day before Christ takes us out of the darkness in this world.

[17] ***Therefore do not be vague and thoughtless and foolish, but understanding and firmly grasping what the will of the Lord is.***

This is crucial. Because of the evil and shortness of time, we might be tempted to spend our days in activity of our own choosing. However, this would include wasted energy. The important thing is to find God's will for each day and do it. This ***understanding*** is a transforming of the mind because of the Word of God, prayer, fellowship with the Holy Spirit, and worship. Yes, there is time to enjoy the blessings of life, but always consider the plans of God for you each day.

Note that it is quite possible to be busy on "Christian work" and be out of the will of the Lord. ***Grasping*** wisdom is to discern God's will, then to obey it.

[18] ***And do not <u>get drunk</u> with wine, for that is debauchery; but ever be filled and stimulated with the [Holy] Spirit.***
(Underline added for emphasis)

Paul makes one of his many contrasts here: Being drunk and out of control vs. being under the Spirit's control.

Concerning wine, there is nothing wrong with Christians who make a stand of *total abstinence*. Many do.

In addition, let us be aware that the Bible was written for believers in all cultures, many in countries where wine is a common beverage on the table. Also in Paul's day, people involved in cults believed that being drunk was a way to be inspired. They theorized that it was only when drunk that they could sense the god of the occult and follow him.

Scriptures do not condemn the *use* of wine—rather they condemn its *abuse*. Paul says specifically **do not get drunk with wine.**

It becomes an abuse:

#1   When it leads to excess (Proverbs 23:30-35)
#2   When it becomes habit-forming (1 Corinthians 6:12b)
#3   When it offends the weak believer (Romans 14:13; 1 Corinthians 8:9)
#4   When it hurts a Christian's testimony in a community (1 Corinthians 10:31)
#5   When there is any doubt in the Christian's mind about it. (Romans 14:23)

Paul recommends an alternative: **But ever be filled and stimulated with the [Holy] Spirit.** He had just commanded his readers to know God's will and to live wisely in v. 17. Now he tells his readers exactly what that is—being filled with the Spirit. He draws the comparison that believers should not be drunk on wine because that leads to excessiveness and being *out of control*. However, he does want them to be "out of control" of themselves and allow the Holy Spirit to control them.

When we receive Christ as our Savior, the Holy Spirit immediately indwells us. That can never be *changed*. Nevertheless, each moment, we must surrender control of our lives to the Holy Spirit. That is the kind of "filling" Paul refers to here. He uses the *present passive imperative* tense of the word **filled**, which means "keep on being filled." If you are submissive to the Holy Spirit allowing Him to control you, you are being filled with the Spirit.

He contrasts the two "fillings," because there are similarities *and* differences.

In both cases, the individual is under an influence: One under wine (it is called *spirits* at times); the other stimulated with the Holy Spirit.

Both cases lead to fervency.

In both cases, the physical condition is affected.

In the case of drunkenness, there is loss of self-control; but the fruit of the Spirit is self-control

Paul concludes with the results of being filled with the Spirit in vv. 19-20. Some of the evidence includes:

> [19] *speak out to one another in psalms and hymns and spiritual songs, offering praise with voices [and instruments] and making melody with all your heart to the Lord,*

This is certainly related to the singing of spiritual songs. This is a picture of a Spirit-filled life that is a fountain bubbling over with joy. Note that Paul says **speak** which is a little confusing. We do not usually *speak* **psalms and hymns and spiritual songs**. However, as we worship our Lord with these various forms, we are indeed *speaking* to **one another** and **the Lord**. I may visit someone and read from Psalms with great joy. *That* I believe fits well in this Scripture.

Paul desired for his readers not to just talk about their faith but to use music as a means of expressing their joy in knowing Jesus. When we are filled with the Spirit, we are able to have attitudes that the world just cannot comprehend, like joyfulness, gratefulness, and willingly submitting ourselves to others. The **spiritual songs** may come forth in songs we know or songs we compose in worship. I have been in gatherings with fellow believers and as we sing our worship, a beautiful unknown song comes forth.

Do not leave v. 19 without noting another result of being filled with the Spirit: The final phrase **making melody with all your heart to the Lord.** The Spirit-filled believer's life is like a fountain of joy springing up from within. **And the disciples were continually filled [throughout their souls] with joy and the Holy Spirit.** (Acts 13:52)

> Being filled with the Spirit will also result in a reigning Spirit of gratitude to God, [20] **At all times and for everything giving thanks in the name of our Lord Jesus Christ to God the Father.**

Not occasional, but continual appreciation to Him; not only for the pleasant things, but also for all things. A believer has a deep appreciation for His Father, and has a spontaneous "outburst" during life's event.

ASK: *How can a believer give thanks to God for everything?*

Joyce Meyer adds, "So often we make mountains out of molehills. We blow things up all out of proportion. We make major issues out of minor situations that are of no real importance whatsoever. We need to learn to adapt, to let things go, to quit allowing our souls to rule our lives. We need to learn to walk by the Spirit and not by the flesh." [28]

It is quite easy to be thankful for sunshine. However, when the clouds of life surround you and when the storms roll in, it takes the filling of the Spirit to be thankful. As I have "matured" (I did not want to say, "as I have grown older"), it has become much easier to thank Him for every event of every day.

Section Six
Additional Questions and Thoughts for Discussion

1. What describes the Gentiles life before knowing Christ? The author listed seven characteristics.
2. How does a new nature replace the old nature? Describe the new nature.
3. What characteristics of the old nature are rejected in the new nature? Why do you think he begins with 'lying'? What does Paul list as 'replacements' for the old nature?
4. Why is 'being out of control' harmful? Yet, what is incorrect about this statement: "I never saw him/her angry with anything?"
5. How can the Holy Spirit be grieved?
6. What are some ways a child imitates his or her parents?
7. Discuss how we can imitate God's love.
8. Discuss the topic of *your words*. As a group, browse through Proverbs looking for Scriptures that relate to what you say.
9. What is the fruit of light?

SEVENTEEN

Heavenly Home

We completed the thoughts of Paul on "Morality of the Believer." He ended his thoughts in vv. 19-20 of cp. 5 with *three* results of being filled with the Spirit:

1. *[19] Speak out to one another in psalms and hymns and spiritual songs.*
2. *offering praise with voices [and instruments] and making melody with all your heart to the Lord,*
3. *[20] At all times and for everything giving thanks in the name of our Lord Jesus Christ to God the Father.*

This is good "stand alone" advice for each one of us. The Holy Spirit is vital to our life!

ASK: *Are you missing one or more of these in worship?*

This next section in Ephesians includes v. 21 of cp. 5 through v. 9 of cp. 6, and concerns **Life at Home and Work of the Believer.**

Many scholars include v. 21 of cp. 5 as a conclusion to the previous section—I do not discover any problem with that. However, I move it to the introduction for this next section. We would suggest it is both the conclusion and introduction to these two sections.

Paul says [21] ***Be subject to one another out of reverence for Christ*** as he begins *the believer's life at home and work.* The results of being filled with the Spirit, worship and giving thanks, naturally lead to working together in the harmony of life.

I believe it was Charles H. Spurgeon who said, "When home is ruled according to God's Word, angels might be asked to stay a night with us, and they would not find themselves out of their element." (Exact source unknown)

The difficulty: Many homes, even homes where the members are Christians, are not governed by God's Word. They do not conform to the three results of being filled with the Spirit.

This next Section emphasizes *submission* and what it means. Paul sites three specific areas in the Christian household where submission is the key.

> Wives and husbands
> Children and parents
> Employees and employers

This topic continues with Paul's previous teaching on unity. We studied Paul's comment [18] ***but ever be filled and stimulated with the [Holy] Spirit.*** That is the answer to all three of these areas he will address. This is God's command and He expects us to obey. The failure rate in family harmony and love is entirely too high. I believe it is only through the power of the Holy Spirit that a husband and wife are able to walk together. Likewise, parents and children, employers and employees walking together underneath this umbrella of submission is a result of the Holy Spirit of God.

Paul made a command, and the verb is in the *present tense* "keep on being filled"—***ever be filled.***

However, the verb is also *passive*, rather than self-initiated. We do not fill ourselves. We permit the Spirit to fill us. The verb "fill" has nothing to do with *contents* or *quantity*, as though we are empty vessels that need a required amount of spiritual fuel to keep going. In the Bible, *filled* usually means "controlled by."

In Acts 13:45 the same word says *the Jews . . . filled with envy.* They were "controlled" by it.

Therefore, Paul applies the whole area of submission, to husband and wives in vv. 21-23, parents and children in cp. 6 vv. 1-4, and to "bosses" and "servants" in vv. 5-9.

Jesus was certainly the one to teach about submission. He *taught* and *lived* it. At the Last Supper the disciples were arguing over who was the greatest (Luke 22:24-27). As Jesus washed their feet, He taught them that the greatest is the person who uses his authority to build up people. We are to esteem others "more important than ourselves" (Romans 12:10; Philippians 2:1-4). By nature, we want to *promote* ourselves, but the Holy Spirit enables us to *submit* ourselves.

[22] *Wives . . .* and [25] *Husbands*

God created the first woman from the side of the first man in Genesis. From their marriage sprang everything else on earth! I agree with Boyce who appropriately says, "Moreover, marriage is the institution from which all other institutions come. The earliest education was done in the home, as mothers and fathers instructed their children to eat, walk, speak, work, and do many other things. From this basic and natural responsibility have come all formal centers for learning: schools, academies, colleges, universities, and other educational organizations. The earliest health care was developed in the home. Then came hospitals, clinics, and hospices. The home was the earliest center of human government. From a father's rightful rule in his home there developed patriarchal, monarchical, and later democratic forms of human rule." [17]

WIVES

[22] *Wives, be subject (be submissive and adapt yourselves) to your own husbands as [a service] to the Lord.* [23] *For the husband is head of the wife as Christ is the Head o the church, Himself the Savior of [His] body.* [24] *As the church is*

subject to Christ, so let wives also be subject in everything to their husbands.

In vv. 22-24 when Paul begins **Wives, *be subject*,** he does not mean become a slave because each party in the marriage is living under the same "Lordship," **Christ.** Paul allowed for no grounds of *abuse* here; instead, he gave us a model of loving and mutual submission that works for each other's good. Any type of competition, pulling rank, selfishness, conceit, domination or deceit are all replaced by this two-way submission that Paul drives home.

I cannot get away from Paul's context in this whole area. *One another* and *out of reverence for Christ* in v. 21 are his main thoughts. Too many marriages have not received this advice given by the Holy Spirit through Paul.

When a Christian wife submits to the Lordship of Christ, she will have little difficulty in submitting to her husband. A marriage is "each for the other, both for Christ." There is nothing more attractive than a woman fulfilling the role, which God has assigned to her. Read Proverbs 31 for the pattern.

Elizabeth George wrote, "Instead of taking care of their own faithfulness to their God-given assignment as wives, they take on the self-appointed role of playing 'Holy Spirit' in their husband's lives, pointing out their faults and shortcomings. These wives may even assume a 'when—then' attitude. In their hearts (and maybe even verbally), they say, '*When* he does this or that, *then* I'll do this or that.' They postpone obedience to their roles as wives and make it conditional to that of their husbands."[28]

That explains why a believer should marry a believer, taught by Paul: *Do not be mismatched with unbelievers.* (2 Corinthians 6:14 HCSB). *Even then,* the roles in marriage have to be understood. Most marital conflicts stem from failure of the husband and/or wife to submit to Christ, spend time in His Word, ask the Holy Spirit for counsel, and seek His will each day. No other way to put it! *but ever be filled and stimulated with the [Holy] Spirit.*

Submission never implies inferiority. It's a decision made in the heart! Read how Paul exalts the wife here comparing her role to the role of the church as the Bride of Christ. No other comparison could be grander. There is nothing inferior insinuated.

Let's note how powerful this area of teaching is. Considering the time of Paul's writing, I imagine a loud, shocking cry would have gone out across the Roman-Greek world with Paul's statements. His instructions were given to believers in Ephesus and across Asia Minor. Many were Romans or Greeks. His statements concerning a Christian's treatment in marriage went against everything Roman and Greek men believed. A husband in that day would never "give himself up for her" as Paul instructs in v. 25. In that day, a man could divorce his wife anytime for any reason. Paul was commanding men to have a very different mind-set—give their wives respect, something they had not enjoyed before.

There is no place for "pulling rank" or "selfishness"—this is [22] *service, as service to the Lord.*

Years ago, my advice in counseling to couples was "if anything's a stumbling block to the wife or husband, change it! There may be nothing wrong with it, but if it causes the other to stumble in your marriage, make a change." It was disturbing how many would "nod" as if in agreement, and then would continue the activity. I still get upset when a husband *or* wife is "stubborn as a mule." Getting one's own way has no place in a marriage. This is a vital word in marriage: *submit.*

HUSBANDS

The husbands are mentioned in vv. 23, 25-33, where Paul says the husband is to be a "preserver" of that unit.

Paul said much more to husbands than he did to wives! Men need more advice and help than women do! I know I do. Paul is holding the husband to a higher standard. The husband is commanded to make Christ's love for the Church, the example of loving his wife. He is never to be selfish and demanding his own way. (1 Corinthians 13)

When Christ is the Lord of the home, the marriage experience is one of constant growth. Love always enlarges and enriches, while selfishness does the opposite.

²⁵ *Husbands, love your wives, as Christ loved the church and gave Himself up for her.* Paul was elevating married love to the highest level possible, for he saw the Christian home as an illustration of the relationship between Christ and the Church! Dare we **ASK:** *Does your home resemble Christ giving His life for His Church through your love for your wife?*

The institution of marriage, even the term, is being questioned and attacked today. Paul makes it clear: Look at Christ's love for His church and imitate *that*:

- He gave Himself for it
- He never sought His own welfare
- He was filled with the Spirit and sought the Father for everything
- He never "used" another for his personal pleasure
- He was a consistent pray-er

God established marriage, *husbands, love your wives,* for many reasons. Among them are:

It meets man's **"emotional"** needs: Genesis 2:18 *It is not good (sufficient, satisfactory) that the man should be alone*. From the beginning, he needed a companion, and "talk" partner.

It has a **"social"** purpose in that children continue the human race.

Certainly, there is a **"physical"** need: God gave a man normal desires to be fulfilled in the marriage, not outside.

In Ephesians, Paul also indicated a **"spiritual"** purpose: In marriage, the husband and wife submit under Christ and His love. (5:22-33)

Someone said that no wife would mind being submissive to a husband who loves her as much as Christ loves the church. Isn't that powerful?

Another man feared he was displeasing God by loving his wife too much! A Christian asked him if he loved her more than Christ loved the church. He responded "no." The Christian responded back, "Only when you go beyond that, do you love your wife too much." **ASK:** *Have you approached the love limit?*

A husband occupies a similar relation to his wife that Christ occupies to the church! That is powerful and should be taught in every marriage-counseling session. *Christ is the Head of the church and He is the*

Savior of [His] body. No wife would be expected to obey her husband if he required her to compromise her loyalty to the Lord. Let me put it this way: If a husband loves and sacrifices himself for the sake of his wife, as Christ did for us, then his wife will joyfully love and sacrifice herself for him in return, as the church does for Jesus.

This word ***Savior*** carries the meaning of Preserver, 1 Timothy 4:10 ***who is the Savior (Preserver, Maintainer, Deliverer) of all men.*** The husband is a preserver as well. As the *head* of the marriage he loves, leads and guides; as *preserver* he provides, protects, and cares. A man's wife is the Queen of their home. She is #1. These are thoughts to counsel every couple who are about to commit their lives together.

Verses 28-29 even go further. If a husband wants to know what this sacrificial love is, he should examine how he cares for his own body. He takes care of it, protects it, provides for it, and *in reality* loves it, [29] ***nourishes and carefully protects and cherishes it.*** Whatever it takes to do this, he does! Husband, meet the needs of your wife!

I have taught many groups on what I called "Leave and Cleave," [31] ***For this reason a man shall leave his father and his mother and shall be joined to his wife, and the two shall become one flesh.*** There comes the point when a man must "leave" parents behind and "cleave" to his bride, forming a new union.

> [33] ***However, let each man of you [without exception] love his wife as [being in a sense] his very own self; and let the wife see that she respects and reverences her husband [that she notices him, regards him, honors him, prefers him, venerates, and esteems him; and that she defers to him, praises him, and loves and admires him exceedingly].*** [1 Peter 3:2.]

Paul summarized this relationship by using two words: ***love*** and ***respect.*** Interestingly, Paul had not used the word ***respect*** before. He said a wife should submit to her husband. When a wife submits to her husband, he feels respected, and that is one of his primary needs because it makes him feel significant. A man needs respect, while a woman needs love.

CHILDREN

Paul continues in another area that demands submission—Children in 6:1-3. Children left alone without discipline—will become rebels. This begins [1] *CHILDREN, OBEY* . . . more submission!

Years ago, the then Duke of Windsor said: "Everything in the American home is controlled by switches . . . . except the children." I have an extensive teaching of Eli (1 Samuel 2), detailing his lack of discipline of his sons, and the tragic result of it.

Fathers are told to "nurture" their children or to help them mature by correcting them in the right manner. This discipline is not in anger but rather in love and encouragement. We also understand, to nurture does not mean to let your children "run over you!" Paul says, "Don't provoke them," rather encourage them and build them up.

There are four reasons that Paul gives for this discipline in those first three verses of cp. 6:

First. [1] *CHILDREN, OBEY your parents in the Lord.* Paul is talking to a family of believers. When one becomes a Christian, he/she is born into a family with rules. Paul has talked about many of these new rules of life *in Christ.*

Actually, one's faith in Christ should make him a better child in the family. He should be taught that submission is what God has set down in the new life. Look at this harmony of the home: The wife submits *as a service to the Lord;* the husband loves his wife *as Christ loved the church;* and the children obey *in the Lord.*

Every society, at least every proper society, rests on two pillars: authority and submission. There must be some who exercise authority and others who submit to that rule. That principle is so basic, it is even found in the Godhead: *But I want you to know that . . . the head of Christ is God.* (1 Corinthians 11:3)

It is not only a plan for human government, but also for the home.

God ordained the place of headship be given to the man. He created man first, then created woman for the man. Both are within this purpose of creation, one with the authority, one with submissiveness.

Second. *For this is just and right.* This is the Divine order that God set down. In setting down the His correct order, in turn it would demand a disciplinary order.

Third. It is one of the Ten Commandments. [2] *Honor (esteem and value as precious) your father and your mother.* Here Paul relates the law to the believer. We do not live under the law, Christ set us free from it (Galatians 3:13 and other New Testament Scriptures). However, the character of God included in the law is a revelation that every believer follows. All of the Ten Commandments are repeated in the New Testament.

Fourth. Paul's final instruction concerning the discipline of children is that it results in blessing, [3] *That all may be well with you and that you may live long on the earth.* When children follow their parent's instruction, much of the sin and difficulties in their life will be avoided. The quality of life, not always the length, will be enriched if this order is followed. Most children are not taught, or do not follow the teaching. Read this area of Scripture to children at an early age. Explain to them "This is God's instruction manual for us." Even then, the Holy Spirit can make these instructions a revelation in the child's life. In fact, Paul did not leave the children out when he commanded *but ever be filled and stimulated with the [Holy] Spirit.* Parents should lead their children *into Christ* at an early age. The Spirit brings peace and harmony to the family.

Somewhere I read these six ways a father can embitter his children:

1. Overprotection
2. Favoritism
3. Discouragement
4. Forgetting a child has ideas of his own and need not be an exact copy of his father
5. Neglect
6. Bitter words and physical cruelty

THE WORKPLACE

The final of three areas Paul considers is the work place in vv. 5-9. Each of the areas he has discussed, have the same principles of faithfulness to each other: Unity, and submission. Many of the principles concerning husbands/wives, parents/children, also apply in this third area. Again, it has this sense of submission because it is performing job-related responsibilities as to God.

> [5] *Servants (slaves), be obedient to those who are your physical masters, having respect for them and eager concern to please them, in singleness of motive and with all your heart, as [service] to Christ [Himself]*

Paul is teaching that no believer is excluded from this submission—those who are free *or* those who are **slaves.** Paul always emphasized that every person in God's eyes is a person of equal worth and value. It is interesting that the Bible does not condone or discourage slavery, for it was an acceptable part of life that even slaves themselves did not question. I believe they would choose freedom if allowed, but they did not think of slavery as immoral. In fact, some slaves purchased slaves for themselves, although all of them belonged to the father of the household. Indeed many slaves were considered a piece of property that the father could do anything with. Yet, within the Roman and Greek cultures, there were limits to the abuse that a master could give a slave. People of the Roman Empire believed work was beneath their dignity. Even the most important duties and positions were filled by slaves, including doctors, teachers, and even those working for the emperor like secretaries. It is obvious that the definition of a slave was different from our concept today.

Paul tells these **servants** to show their serving of Christ through a willingness to serve their masters. As a result, God will reward them [8b] **he will receive his reward from the Lord, whether he is slave or free.**

He seems to be concerned about their attitude in this matter [6] ***Not in the way of eye-service [as if they were watching you] and only to please men, but as servants (employees) of Christ, doing the will of God heartily and with your whole soul.*** Are they serving just to look good and gain their freedom, or sincerely striving to do well for those in authority over them? It is quite easy to slack off when the boss is not looking, but *our* Master is always looking. I think this is summed up in ***doing the will of God with your whole soul.***

Have respect and please your employer, as a service to Christ. Of course, this is a little hard to receive at times, but the Bible is clear.

> [7] *Rendering service readily with goodwill, as to the Lord and not to men,* [8] *Knowing that for whatever good anyone does, he will receive his reward from the Lord, whether he is slave or free.*

Concerning each of the three areas, Paul never said anything about any one of them being easy. To serve ***with goodwill*** is difficult if the master is overbearing, abusive and unreasonable. However, the work can still be done, ***as to the Lord and not to men.*** He is the One who will indeed ***reward.*** This area is what speaks the loudest from your life! The character of life, whether a husband, wife, child, parent or employee, is a Spirit-filled life 24/7. I question the spiritual status of a good employee who comes home and becomes an abusive or disagreeable husband and father. The same thought can be made concerning a wife.

Moreover, the masters/employers should be guided by the same principles of fairness and honesty.

> [9] *You masters, (you employers) act on the same [principle] toward them (your employees) and give up threatening and using violent and abusive words, knowing that He Who is <u>both their Master and yours is in heaven,</u> and that there is no respect of persons (no partiality) with Him.* (Underline added for emphasis)

So, even these masters, have *a master* in heaven.

Section Seven
Additional Questions and Thoughts for Discussion

1. How does being filled with the Spirit relate to a relationship between husband and wife, parents and children, and employee and employer?
2. How can you be continuously filled with the Spirit?

3. Discuss what it means to be submissive. How does being submissive relate to harmony?
4. Is it easy for you to submit to another? Why? Why not? How do I change this?
5. Discuss: A man needs respect—a woman needs love. Do you agree?
6. Do you think Paul's word "submit" to a wife, is understood today?
7. What are some ways a husband misinterprets Paul's teaching? Is there any place for self-centeredness in a marriage?
8. Discuss the relationship of wife-Christ; husband-Chirst.
9. Do you ever 'stir up anger' in your household? Specifics.
10. Relate the slave-master concept to employer-employee of our day.
11. Should an employee work as though he or she is working for the Lord? Discuss how this is possible or impossible.

EIGHTEEN

Battleground

We begin the eighth and final section of Ephesians, which covers vv. 10-24 of cp. 6. This section is entitled the **Warfare and the Believer.** Paul is coming to the close of his letter in v. 10 *In conclusion*. He addresses all the family of God, whether they were Jews or Gentiles, and makes a stirring appeal to them as soldiers of Christ in battle. He includes the specific ones he spoke to: Husbands, wives, parents, children, employees, and employers.

> [10] *In conclusion, be strong in the Lord [be empowered through your union with Him]; draw your strength from Him [that strength which His boundless might provides].*

It is difficult to use a single word to express the full Greek emphasis concerning the anticipation of what he is about to write. The KJV and several other translations read *finally*. To appreciate this, we have to look at the Greek. This is the most important word in the paragraph!

In the Greek, it is the word *loipou (lay po')*. We read it as *in conclusion* or *finally*—and it expresses what will follow is so important that it is held until the very end in order for it to be *emphasized*. What follows is to be remembered as though it is the only topic you recall! Paul used the same word when earlier he wrote Philippians 3:1, *FOR THE rest, my brethren*. Even there it is evident he implied "pay attention to what I'm about to write".

He is saying, "Let this paragraph be digested." This is remarkable when we glance at what Paul has taught in this letter. Let me summarize by using a thought from Rick Renner:

> "He taught about the election of the saints (1:4)
> The predestination work of God (1:5)
> The adoption of the sons of God (1:5)
> The sealing of the Holy Spirit (1:13)
> The earnest of the Holy Spirit (1:14)
> The power of God that is available to every believer (1:19)
> The grace of God (2:1-10)
> The eternal plan of God (3:10-11)
> The fivefold ministry gifts (4:11-13)
> The infilling with the Spirit (5:18-19)
>
> And the list goes on!"[29]

Yet when we come to the end of this epistle, which is packed, with both of the teachings from the two themes, **Position** *and* **Practice**, Paul says, "Pay attention to *this* if you only remember one thought. *Most of all* remember what I'm about to say."

A BATTLE RAGES

The hosts of Satan are committed to hinder and obstruct the work of Christ. In *our own* strength, we are no match for the devil. Satan has us in the crosshairs of his scope. He studies each one of us.

He knows our background, he is familiar with our vulnerabilities, and he is well acquainted with our weaknesses and strengths. In addition, he takes advantage of it all—to lay snares in our path.

Paul says **_be strong_**, which assures us that a *source* of strength *is available*. The same words indicate that an explosive *dunamis* ability has a receptacle to be placed into, **_be strong_**. The receptacle is you along with every believer! In addition, it is **_in the Lord_**. If we would read the beginning of this letter again, Paul wanted believers to know **_the immeasurable greatness of His power_** and **_the working of His vast strength,_** (1:19 HCSB).

We have to know our enemy and the battle that is raging. He is strong, but the power that raised Christ from the dead is the same power in every believer! Notice the urging **to stand** *four* times:

> [11] *Put on God's whole armor, that you may be able successfully to <u>stand up</u> against the strategies and the deceits of the devil.*
> [13] *Therefore put on God's complete armor, that you may be able to resist and <u>stand your ground</u> on the evil day, and, having done all, <u>to stand</u> [firmly in your place]*
> [14] <u>***Stand therefore.***</u> (Underline added for emphasis)

<u>The Holy Spirit makes it clear, you have to make a stand, and when you do, there is supernatural help!</u> In this spiritual battle, we stand our ground. We need to focus on what God has said in His Word and the truths He has revealed. This study on Ephesians has given us promises to stand on. Do not become off balanced and weak in your stand—you might fall down.

So we are told to be strong in Christ, get ready for battle, and do it by putting on *all* the ***armor,*** in order to stand. He begins with imperative words ***put on.*** These words are a single word in the Greek meaning "empowered" or "endued." This is a command in the Greek, to every child of God. *We* make the choice because God does not dress us. As we walk with Him, His power is *with* and *in* us. The clothing is ours.

> [11] *Put on God's <u>whole</u> armor [the armor of a heavy-armed soldier which God supplies], that you may be able successfully to <u>stand up</u> against [all] the strategies and the deceits of the devil.* (Underline added for emphasis)

Therefore, we put on ***God's <u>whole</u> armor***, to stand in victory over *everything* the enemy sends our way. This battle is a spiritual battle, and only spiritual armor can protect us.

> If the enemy were bacteria, our defense might be penicillin.

> If the enemy were an army, we might mount our defense with guns and tanks.

However, when the enemy is the Devil, our only defense is the spiritual armor of God.

We do not have to continue in the war without having information about the enemy. In any battle, research determines the plan of attack in preparation for the conflict. There is no panic or fear when discussing our enemy. Be assured we know many things about him.

> [12] *For we are not wrestling with flesh and blood [contending only with physical opponents], but against the despotisms, against the powers, against the world rulers of this present darkness, against the spirit forces of wickedness in the heavenly (supernatural) sphere.*

The name devil means accuser
The name Satan means adversary

Earlier I listed many of the names of our enemy. Here are a few more to understand his evil character:

We know this enemy is a *murderer* and a *liar* (John 8:44), compared to a *lion roaring* (1 Peter 5:8), *dragon and serpent* (Revelation 12:9), *an angel of light* (2 Corinthians 11:13-15) as well as the *god of this world* (2 Corinthians 4:4). In addition, he goes before the very throne of God this day as *the seducer of all humanity* to bring accusations against you (Revelation 12:7-11).

We also know our enemy has many helpers. Read again how Paul describes them in v. 12. A definite army scattered around every part of this earth. [12] *For our struggle is not against flesh and blood, but against the rulers, against the powers, against the world forces of this darkness, against the spiritual forces of wickedness in the heavenly places.* (NASU)

We are told about Satan's abilities. We visualize a strong enemy in vv. 10-12 with many *strategies and deceits.* The NASB reads *schemes;* the HCSB reads *tactics;* the KJV has it *wiles.* I list these to emphasize Satan's method of attack. *He is not compared to a lion and a dragon just for fun!*

He has the ability to destroy a man's body, home, wealth, and friends; Jesus said concerning him *the thief comes <u>only</u> in order to steal, and kill, and destroy.* (John 10:10).

Before we summarize the spiritual armor that is available for every believer, let me quickly give you *four* principles to stand on against Satan and his entire hierarchy. Think about them:

> #1 God is stronger than any attack from Satan
> #2 God's armor can deflect any of Satan's schemes
> #3 God's work will continue
> #4 A believer's prayers will prevail over Satan

So God gives us armor. We know our enemy, we know his helpers and Paul details our battle gear we have to stand against that enemy. Let's learn about the *seven* pieces of armor from vv. 13-18. Notice what Paul says in v.10: God's *full armor.* We are to put on all of God's available armor. Do not leave any weak areas uncovered for the enemy. We must not be selective. As we will see, Paul begins with a belt of the Truth, which is God's Word. If anything protects us from being "up and down" in winds of doctrine, it is this belt. Our spiritual "backbone" will be strengthened to stand tall and straight and do the right thing. Most of our armor "hangs" on the belt.

We have this armor to stand in victory against him because he has [11] *strategies and deceits.*

These words *strategies and deceits* show a plural attack; they show us that Satan has more than one method of attack. The Greek has only a single word, but it is plural. The word here is strongly connected to "thoughts and purposes."

Paul did not want us to be ignorant of the fact that Satan has his sights set on our minds. In fact as you read again vv. 10—13 in the various translations, you will notice the battlefield against the enemy, *is the mind.*

He will use whatever mind schemes he has to draw you away from God. Whether it is unresolved conflicts with another or bitterness towards anyone, he *will* use it on you!

Learn about each piece of armor. If you put on the helmet, and leave off the breastplate, guess what? You might be killed during battle from the enemy's arrows, sword, or lance.

If you protect your mid-section and have bare feet, you will not be able to **stand** during the battle. As you advance, you might step on a sharp unseen object and fall.

Put it *all* on. Nothing less than **God's whole armor** will do.

THE ENEMY'S FORCES

The organized armies of Satan are mentioned in v. 12. Understand that there are indeed many devils with individual responsibilities and assignments. Some live in dark, gloomy slums—others move around just looking for someone to attack with anything discovered as a weakness. Our enemy's command of his forces is not one of chaos or weakness. It is made up of an organized hierarchy of strength. Paul speaks of the unseen governmental setup established by Satan. He lists the armies as **despotisms, powers, world rulers of this present darkness, and spirit forces of wickedness in the heavenly sphere**.

I understand this to be "from top to bottom" in Satan's domain. I conclude this as a result of examining the Greek words Paul used.

The **first** word used is **despotisms** taken from the Greek word *archas*. The KJV uses the familiar "principalities." The NASU has it "rulers." This is an old word meaning the *chief rank* in matters of order. It is also used when referring to individuals who hold the *highest position* or rank. I believe Paul is saying the **despotisms** hold the highest position of power in Satan's (Lucifer's) government.

The **next** group Paul calls **powers,** just below the **despotisms.** This word is from the Greek word *exousia* and makes it clear that this group has received *delegated authority*, indicating a slightly lower level. Apparently, this level is *second in command* and has authority to carry out whatever form of attack *they* choose. They act on behalf of Satan with a high degree of control received from him.

Continuing to list the rank and file of this dark kingdom, Paul includes **world rulers of this present darkness.** This is an interesting phrase taken from the Greek *kosmokratoras*. It actually is a combination of two words, the familiar word *kosmos*, meaning orderly arrangement of inhabitants, and *krateo* having to do with organized strength or power to seize. The resulting compounded word depicts power put in a range of order. The resulting word *kosmokratoras* was used to picture a military facility where men were brought together and trained, creating a powerful army. From this, we can conclude that Satan has some higher ranked fallen angels who are assigned to possibly train the other ranks for specific attacks!

ASK: *What does this mean for you and me?*

I would suggest that every believer realize Satan has a gigantic army to destroy you. He has various squads sent forth with assignments designed to destroy human beings, particularly God's children.

The **final** group mentioned by Paul is more of the *character* of Satan's entire army, *spirit forces of wickedness in the heavenly (supernatural) sphere.* This is the "spirit" they go forth with! *Wickedness* is taken from the Greek *poneros* depicting any attack that is "vicious, vile or bad." All evil spirits are specifically sent forth to attack us is various ways. Not only is this a specific group, but this phrase reveals Satan's ultimate goal: Destroy us.

Dangerous? Yes. Powerful? Yes. However, we note here that any believer, who is filled with the power of the Holy Spirit, can overcome all the *strategies and the deceits* of the enemy's entire force! We have the Greater One living inside us. Never begin a day without knowing this.

What are these *strategies and the deceits of the devil?* As mentioned, they generally start in the mind. For example, unforgiveness, envy, lack of spiritual knowledge, doubt and fear are all methods used by Satan's army. Do not allow any of these fiery darts to stick in you. If these are not dealt with, they create additional openings for the enemy to gain a foothold.

Paul knew what an attack against the mind was. In 2 Corinthians 2:10-11 Paul said he lived at all times in forgiveness of anyone, so that no advantage would be taken of him by Satan, *for we are not ignorant of his wiles and intentions.*

So what is *our war strategy* to be? How can we prepare for Satan's attacks on our minds? We have to assemble the right weapons. These are spiritual weapons offered by God. *Know them.*

The war is not against godless philosophers or unsaved neighbors. It is not against cult followers or infidel rulers. I repeat that our war is against the unseen hierarchy of unseen satanic beings. They can *not* indwell in you as a strong believer, but they *can* oppress and harass you in different degrees!

In the armor provided by God Himself, which Paul is about to list, you have all that is needed to hold your ground against the foe.

From the highest ***Principalities*** on downward to the ***Powers***, on to the ***Rulers of the darkness of this age***, right to the bottom, the ***spiritual hosts of wickedness in the heavenly places,*** our enemy is organized for war! (From the NKJV)

They are organized to *kill, steal and destroy* everything about you and me.

That is why you have the armor of God!

Nineteen

God's Armor

Verses 13-18 list seven pieces of a soldier's armor. Paul uses the Roman soldier to explain our spiritual armor that we put on.

13 Therefore put on God's complete armor, that you may be able to resist and stand your ground on the evil day [of danger], and, having done all [the crisis demands], to stand [firmly in your place].

14 Stand therefore [hold your ground], having tightened the belt of <u>truth</u> around your loins and having put on the breastplate of <u>integrity</u> and of moral rectitude and right standing with God,

15 And having shod your feet in preparation [to face the enemy with the firm-footed stability, the promptness, and the readiness produced by the good news] of the Gospel of <u>peace</u>.

16 Lift up over all the [covering] shield of saving <u>faith</u>, upon which you can quench all the flaming missiles of the wicked [one].

17 And take the helmet of <u>salvation</u> and the sword that the Spirit wields, which is the <u>Word of God</u>.

18 <u>Pray</u> at all times (on every occasion, in every season) in the Spirit, with all [manner of] prayer and entreaty. To that end keep alert and watch with strong purpose and perseverance, interceding in behalf of all the saints (God's consecrated people). (Underlines added for emphasis)

I never saw this as clear until I prepared this last chapter: We win the battle with **truth, integrity, peace, faith, salvation, Word of God and prayer.** Read these again, they are your armor.

We must exercise them, in order to stand. Paul uses something physical, which they were familiar with, to drive home these mighty spiritual truths.

We *learn* about these seven armaments, and place them *on* by faith. We do not wake up in the morning and physically reach out to put on our armor.

Paul was familiar with the Roman soldier's armor. During much of his time in prisons, he was chained to a Roman soldier.

> He *saw* the armor
> He was *affected* by it
> At times, he *looked* at it out through prison bars!
> Paul was an "expert" in all the pieces of a Roman soldier's dress.

Paul uses the Roman soldier's armor in admonishing every believer to put on **God's** armor. No believer escapes spiritual warfare; however in putting on the spiritual armor, he will be victorious.

He lists a *belt of truth*, *breastplate of integrity* (righteousness), a *gospel of peace*, *shield of faith*, *helmet of salvation* and a *sword the Spirit wields*. As we will see, everything works around an added weapon, *pray at all times*.

TRUTH

#1 Strap Tight the Belt of Truth *having tightened the belt of <u>truth</u>* (Underline added for emphasis)

Psalm 40:11-12 *Withhold not Your tender mercy from me, O Lord; let Your loving-kindness and Your truth continually preserve me!* [12] *For innumerable evils have compassed me about.*

Two things to know concerning truth: *Walk* with truth in everything you do and say, and walk in *the* Truth of the Word of God, our Bible.

I want you to understand what he says concerning each of the pieces of armor.

The *belt* on a Roman soldier's uniform did a lot more than match his pants and hold them up! I have left home for an engagement, and forgot a belt. It wasn't pretty! This makes the first piece of armor perhaps *the most important of all the armor*. A belt (or *loinbelt* as several translations read) was almost unnoticed. Most of the soldier's armor was beautiful: The helmet, usually vibrantly painted; a bright and shiny breastplate—everyone loved that glistening sword! Even the sandals with spikes on the bottom, leather straps up to the knees. Perhaps you have seen pictures of a Roman soldier, fully dressed in his armor. Quite attractive. However, almost no one ever notices the belt. Yet, it was vital.

The Roman soldier's loinbelt was the piece of armor that held all the other pieces together. I would say it was important! On one side, his sword hung in a scabbard that was attached to the side of his loinbelt. When not in use, his small shield could be hung on a special clip on the other side of his loinbelt. The pouch that carried his arrows rested on a small ledge attached to his loinbelt on his backside. The belt wrapped even his breastplate that was two pieces, one down the front, the other the back, tightly. The soldier wore a loose skirt that hung to his knees, which he would tuck under his belt during combat so the loose folds would not prevent his movement.

To tighten **the belt around your waist** meant you were prepared for battle.

For the believer, it is truth, honesty, sincerity—the **gospel of truth** that makes you prepared for spiritual battle.

Our lives—must *be* truth and ruled *by* it! John 14:6 says Jesus is **the truth** and the belt worn by every believer must be the whole truth of God in His Word.

No phony fronts, no hypocrisy, no doubts. No hope, assumptions, or allowing another to interpret the truth or the Bible for you. Your life is to be *truth*.

As you face the enemy in a fierce battle, flaming words of anger may be flying towards you, words are bursting all around—it is very tempting to run from battle by retreating into a lie or what we mistakenly call "stretching the truth" or "white lie".

It may seem so much easier or safer to allow a false statement to stand. Always remember the belt is Truth—Jesus is Truth. That is why Paul urged us to keep that belt pulled tight, not to loosen the truth. We are Christ's representatives.

To have all His armor, we must *begin* and *finish* by walking in the truth of His Word. Therefore, as you go about your daily routine today and every day, keep your "loinbelt of truth" fully attached and operative in every situation you face. Let the Bible be the governor, the law, the ruler, the "final say-so" in your life!

RIGHTEOUSNESS

#2 Protect Your Life With The Breastplate of Righteousness, *having put on the breastplate of* <u>integrity</u> *and of moral rectitude and right standing with God.* (Underline added for emphasis)

Righteousness protects the heart—Proverbs 13:6: ***"Righteousness guards him whose way is blameless . . . but wickedness overthrows the sinner."*** Walk in the righteousness that is yours—He made you righteous, know it, walk it, and live it.

The Roman breastplate was a large double-piece of metal that covered both the back and front of a soldier from his neck to his thighs.

It protected the heart and vital organs and was an essential piece of armor. No soldier would go to battle without this piece. It was always inspected to assure it had not been weakened in a previous battle, always made ready for battle. In fact, the enemy would always hope for a weak point in the breastplate to drive their sword through.

Solomon put it this way: ***Keep and guard your heart with all vigilance and above all that you guard, for out of it flow the springs of life.*** (Proverbs 4:23). That is our breastplate of righteousness.

What you have in your heart determines your thoughts. Your thoughts determine your speech. Your speech determines your integrity. The battle with the enemy is generally fought on the battleground of the mind. Everything we do comes by thought. If our thoughts come from His Word, we win. If the thoughts are from the flesh or the world, we lose.

I like what Paul adds in 1 Thessalonians 5:8 ***the breastplate of faith and love.***

This breastplate is not made of works of a religious testimony that only produce emptiness. *That* righteousness would never withstand the blows of the enemy. It would be a breastplate full of holes and weak spots. God is after faith that works by love. *That* righteousness will withstand the arrows.

Righteousness is our breastplate because it assures us that we have been made right with God through the blood of Jesus. You can have faith in that! 2 Corinthians 5:21 assures us ***in and through Him we might become the righteousness of God.***

Know it. Put it on. We put on each piece of armor by knowing what it is and walking with it.

Theologians describe this as *positional* or *imputed* righteousness. Know that you were made the righteousness of God; He imparted that to you, when you accepted Christ. Your position *in Christ* is as though you never committed a sin. You are made righteous by what Jesus Christ did for you. God looks at you behind this breastplate.

Righteousness is as essential to us as the Roman soldier's breastplate was to him. Our enemy loves to sling his arrows at the heart of our faith. He would like to pierce your life with his lies.

When we stand firm in the knowledge that Christ has declared us righteous, the enemy must retreat in defeat.

PEACE

#3 Step in to Sandals of Peace [15] ***And having shod your feet in preparation [to face the enemy with the firm-footed stability, the promptness, and the readiness produced by the good news] of the Gospel of peace.*** (Underline added for emphasis)

Isaiah 40:9 ***O you who bring good tidings to Zion, get up to the high mountain. O you who bring good tidings to Jerusalem, lift up your voice with strength, lift it up, be not afraid; say to the cities of Judah, Behold your God!***

The footwear of the soldier in that day was not some "flimsy" sandal—not some "beach sandal" that we would wear today. The Roman soldier wore an open-toed leather boot strapped up to the mid calf and having a nail-studded sole, tied to the ankles and shins with leather straps. Many times these included "grieves," a metal covering for the shin. Paul uses this shoe or sandal to explain *peace.*

Peace just gives us a firm stand with *all* the other armaments.

It is obvious soldiers were not used to fleeing *from* or running *towards* the enemy. The spiked-boots provided the soldier with mobility and ability to travel on long marches over difficult ground. They also provided protection from injury that would keep the soldier from taking a firm stand in battle. An enemy many times would bury sharp objects on the battlefield with the intent of bringing the soldier to a halt. Also, as a soldier walked through the thorns and thistles of the wild brush, the grieves would protect from cuts.

Many times the battle included hand-to-hand combat! The soldier could dig in for battle with those spikes, which would have been similar to football cleats.

We must have that same security and sure footing in our spiritual stand. Our "footing" or "standing" is our peace with God. It is protection in times of need. Peace with God and with each other. When we feel we are "slipping" in matters of life, we reflect on what Christ has done for us and allow peace to rule. This peace restores our sure footing once again. Note this verse is not speaking of spreading the gospel, because vv. 10-16 pictures believers standing strong rather than advancing into a battle. This is the believer's surefootedness because of the gospel, which gives him peace to stand in the battle.

Satan may push all that he wants in trying to convince us that God will reject and judge us when we mess up. If we know that we have peace from God and we are wearing our sandals or boots, we will not slip and fall. *Contentment always stands with confidence.*

Our stand in being ready for battle is to wear the gospel of peace no matter how the battle progresses. If we have the gospel of peace in our hearts, we are ready to go, to be, to do, and to say, whatever the battle demands.

We have the power to impart peace wherever we go.

When Jesus sent His disciples out to preach for the first time, He said in Matthew 10:13: *Then if indeed that house is deserving, let come upon it your peace [that is, freedom from all the distresses that are experienced as the result of sin]. But if it is not deserving, let your peace return to you.*

FAITH

#4 Lift Up the Shield of Faith shield *of saving _faith_,*
(Underline added for emphasis)

This is a *delivering* faith.

> 1 Samuel 17:45-46 *Then said David to the Philistine, You come to me with a sword, a spear, and a javelin, but I come to you in the name of the Lord of hosts, the God of the ranks of Israel, Whom you have defied.* [46] *This day the Lord will deliver you into my hand*

The Roman soldier owned two kinds of shields. One was a small circular shield used in hand-to-hand combat. The other, referred to by Paul, was a long rectangular shield that he could stand behind. It was four feet tall and two and a half feet wide. Paul perhaps noticed the Roman soldiers would prop their shield up against a wall throughout the day.

This large shield was covered with leather, and soaked in water prior to battle; the water would put out the enemies flaming arrows when they hit the shield. In Paul's days, the enemy's arrows were often dipped in a flammable liquid and set on fire. The arrows *still came* and stuck, but they were quickly put out!

Paul knew this is exactly what could happen to a believer if he lowered his spiritual shield as Satan attacked with flaming darts. If your shield of faith has slipped, perhaps because of anger or depression, the enemy's flaming arrows will get to you. As mentioned earlier, our enemy's flaming arrows take many other forms: doubt, pride, despair, fear, guilt shame, and confusion. Many times his darts are disguised as rational thoughts. Things that make sense are not always truth.

David in a time of discouragement said *For You, Lord, will bless the [uncompromisingly] righteous [him who is upright and in right standing with You]; as with a shield You will surround him with goodwill (pleasure and favor)* Psalm 5:12. He too was referring to the large shield covering the entire body. His song closed by asking God to take his inner anxiety and replace it with joy. He was exercising faith, *You will surround him.*

Paul is telling us our faith should be similar to this huge protective shield. It will protect us at all angles. It was made in such a way as to join another soldier's faith and form a solid wall of safety. At times, the battle shields would be locked together with other shields to form a wall in front and overhead. I do not visualize a soldier running to another *every time* the enemy attacked. Rather he would make his own stand. God wants each of us to mature and many times fight the battle ourselves. However when the enemy's force is bringing too much pressure, soldiers would join with each other to stand. Matthew 18:20 *For wherever two or three are gathered (drawn together as My followers) in (into) My name, there I AM in the midst of them.*

The enemy will try to trip your spouse or your children. He will try to trip you in your health, your finances, or your emotions. He will shower you with doubts, questions, suggestions, imaginations, desires and lusts to cause you to fall into fear, the opposite of faith.

What you need is a shield of faith to quickly extinguish all these darts. It needs to be big enough for you and every member of your family to stand behind. Of course, this does not mean you are the only soldier in the family with faith. Each one has a shield.

Any of those darts ever fly towards you? **ASK:** *Can you recall when fire came towards you?* Arrows *will* come—they *will stick*, but will quickly be extinguished because you walk by faith! You are a faith man—you are a faith woman. The water of the Word *and* your faith equal victory.

By faith, you and I trust in God. See life, love, and peace, through God's eyes. Then stand safely behind the mighty shield!

SALVATION

#5 Put on the Helmet of Salvation [17] *And take the helmet of salvation* (Underline added for emphasis)

2 Chronicles 6:41 So ***now arise, O Lord God, and come into Your resting place, You and the ark of Your strength and power. Let Your priests, O Lord God, be clothed with salvation, and let Your saints (Your zealous ones) rejoice in good and in Your goodness.***

Understand the word *salvation* in the Scriptures. Many years ago, I wrote a note in the margin of my Bible beside Isaiah 12:2-3. The Scripture reads [2] ***Behold, God is my salvation; I will trust, and not be afraid: for the Lord JEHOVAH is my strength and my song; he also is become my salvation.*** [3] ***Therefore with joy shall ye draw water out of the <u>wells of salvation</u>.*** (KJV)

> My note in the margin still can be read even though it has faded over the years: "Salvation is an all-inclusive word in the Hebrew. It includes health, deliverance, safety, victory, defense and prosperity. There are many wells for you and me to draw from. Many have drawn from only one well. The remaining wells aren't putting forth any benefit at all."

> In research for this book and digging further into the Hebrew for salvation, I concluded that my note of some thirty years ago—still stands.

The spiritual warfare that Satan wages for your soul begins "in the head." Satan would like to have his arrows strike our minds. He would count it a victory if a believer would fall from the hope and assurance of our eternal life in Christ. A soldier wounded in the head is instantly useless even though he may be alive. He cannot make good decisions. We saw how the breastplate guards our hearts, which is important. If the heart is damaged it is certainly serious. However, our minds are essential for staying alive. The body may survive, but it is not much of a life without the brain. We could be spiritually dead if we do not protect our knowledge from the doubts of the enemy.

The Roman helmet was carefully custom crafted for each soldier. Paul says to *"take the helmet of salvation"* for the helmet protected the entire head. The brass or iron plates protected the cheeks, a band the forehead.

You are wounded in your head when your thoughts are negative and suspicious. Perhaps your imaginations are vulgar and sensual. This is like removing a helmet in battle! Remove it by thoughts of evil or doubt and the enemy goes for a deathblow.

That's why 2 Corinthians 10:5 says *We are destroying speculations and every lofty thing raised up against the knowledge of God, and we are taking every thought captive to the obedience of Christ,*

And remember, Jesus said *"take no thought . . . saying . . . ."*

Our salvation, quite appropriately is the helmet, shielding our minds from Satan's attack. He would love to convince you that you really do not belong to God. "Am I really saved?" "Is His Word really working for me?" Your helmet is what protects you from Satan's lies. His attempt is to steal any hope you might have of an eternal home with God. He would attempt to kill your confidence in having a victory over all the enemy's forces.

When you find yourself thinking about something that is not of God, refer to the helmet of your salvation in Christ, which brings renewal and wholeness. Just say, "I have the mind of Christ, and I will NOT think about such trash!"

Your assurance is in your salvation. Nothing can snatch you out of Christ's hands *and* His thoughts!

#6 Wield the Sword of the Spirit *the sword that the Spirit wields*

Jeremiah 23:29 *Is not My word like fire [that consumes all that cannot endure the test]? says the Lord, and like a hammer that breaks in pieces the rock [of most stubborn resistance]?*

The sword is designed for offence, for attacking the enemy. Do not run from him, plunge the word of God into his belly.

The Roman soldier's sword was designed for attacking, not for defending. So far, all the armor has been defensive. Too often, we think the whole battle with the enemy is "being on the defensive."

To some extent, it is true. However, don't *ever* think you are not to retaliate, to return fiery darts of your own. Just read Romans 12:7-21 for how we are to respond in life to others.

Our single offensive weapon is God's word of truth! *"and take . . . . the sword that the Spirit wields, which is the word of God."* This is the *only piece* of armor that Paul details in this passage. It *is the word of God*. Every other piece of armor has already been explained in Ephesians. The belt of *Truth* was in 4:25, breastplate of *righteousness* in 5:3, sandal of *peace* in 2:14, shield of *faith* in 3:20, and helmet of *salvation* in 2:8.

There are two Greek words for the Word of God. *Logos* means the written Word of God and *rhema* means the spoken Word of God. Paul uses *rhema* in this Ephesians passage. *Logos* is the more familiar word to many of us. Indeed it is powerful, as it refers to God's ordering of all principles of the world. This is the word John used in his Gospel (1:1, 4). To John, *Logos* was Jesus Christ being God's final Word to all people. *Rhema,* the word used in our passage, is not referring to "everything." *Rhema* carries the meaning of "a saying" or specific part of Logos. Each verse we read or quote is a *rhema*. I like to refer to a specific Scripture as *"a rhema word."* Paul says our sword is the specific Scripture we stand on and strike the enemy with.

Satan is not afraid of *Logos*; he knows what it is. However, he runs away like a mouse from *rhema*. This is what Jesus used in the wilderness. It is so powerful that when Jesus was in the wilderness and tempted by the devil, He answered every temptation with the *rhema* Word of God. Matthew 4:4 *but by every word* (*rhema*) that *comes forth from the mouth of God.*

When Jesus quoted from the Book of Deuteronomy, Satan misquoted it back to Jesus from Psalm 91. If Satan twisted Scripture with Jesus, he will twist it with you.

It is sharp and powerful to pierce the soul and discern even the thoughts and intents of our hearts.

Satan never questioned the authority of the Word of God. Nevertheless, what he tries to do is twist it to bring doubt into your mind. **Doubt kills faith, and faith kills doubt.**

Many times I think of *"a rhema word"* as **the sharp two-edged sword of Revelation 2:12.** One edge is the Scripture in written form, which is sharp and powerful itself. When the Word of God is released *from the* *mouth of a believer* it becomes *two* sided and Satan *will* flee. Keep in mind: Nothing will happen in your battle with Satan until you speak the living Word of God to him.

The Holy Spirit *anoints* it and Satan is conquered *by it.* There is nothing as powerful as the Word of God. Study it, read it, memorize it. It is alive! (Hebrews 4:12)

Armament #7: Yell out the Battle Cry of Prayer

Paul added one last element, one that reminds us it is in God's strength we do battle, not ours. This must be a part of the complete armor, even though Paul does not relate it to any particular piece. David did say in 1 Samuel 17:45 *You come to me with a sword, a spear, and a javelin.* So perhaps we could use the *spear and javelin* as the armor representing *prayer.*

Prayer expresses our reliance on God. Paul makes it clear:

> [18] *Pray at all times (on every occasion, in every season)* **in the Spirit,** *with all [manner of] prayer*

Remember, our enemy studies our every weakness, and plots his attack accordingly. Therefore, we need to be just as precise when we go to our Father. Prayer must be a central part of our spiritual armor.

There are different types of prayer, (That's a study in itself). Suffice it to say, be specific and be fervent in your talk with God. Pray for others and yourself.

But how often? The Greek word helps us to answer the question. *At all times* is a Greek phrase *"en panti kairo"* indicating *at each and every occasion.* Therefore, we are to pray every possible moment of the day! Don't "only" search for a time to get alone with God (although that too is included)—rather be in an attitude of prayer in every moment. Prayer is to be a part of our life, not only for those who are "gifted" at it. *Prayer is not mentioned in any of the gifts of the Spirit.* That is simply because it is not a gift. It is a *responsibility* of *every* believer. Be a person of prayer. In addition, do not limit the prayer time to clock time. Consistency is needed because the enemy is consistently shooting the arrows!

Paul adds *in the Spirit.* We need the Spirit's help to know how to pray. Even to have the strength to pray, we need the Holy Spirit. Worship, praise, and adoration are included in *with all prayer.* Our prayer becomes selfish and out of God's will if not done *in the Spirit.*

¹⁸ᵇ *To that end keep alert and watch with strong purpose and perseverance*

Pay attention, have your eyes attentive to detect the missiles coming towards you. Be aware of your surroundings. Every soldier was aware that his own life and at times the life of fellow-soldiers, was at stake. The soldier would concentrate on being *alert.* Even if it takes longer than you like, or think, keep on keeping on. Examine your life for darts coming your way. We see also the word *perseverance* in v. 18. It means, "don't quit." We want the Spirit's will and will not quit until God answers.

We read *interceding in behalf of all the saints (God's consecrated people).*

We are all targets of Satan's fiery arrows, from the most mature to the new born. No one outgrows the need for a united front against the enemy. We pray together as a family, each for the other. Paul asks prayer for himself in the next verse.

Paul's closing comments and personal request are in the last six verses of the letter.

He makes a personal request in v. 19 *And [pray] also for me.* Paul was aware of his need to receive prayer.

Paul was writing the Ephesians letter from home-captivity, but you will notice he did not ask prayer to be released. Rather he asked *that [freedom of] utterance may be given me, that I may open my mouth to proclaim boldly the mystery of the good news.*

Again, Paul mentions the mystery, which he opened the letter with, revealed it throughout the letter, and now comes full circle by mentioning for the last time, in his closing.

Here it is mentioned as the reason for his bonds, but with no regrets. In fact, he wants to proclaim it more and more. That is what he wants them to pray for!

> ²⁰ *For which I am an ambassador in a coupling chain [in prison. Pray] that I may declare it boldly and courageously, as I ought to do*

Ambassadors are generally granted diplomatic immunity from arrest. But not when it comes to the gospel. The gospel stirs up, wherever, whenever it is presented. We see Paul, an ambassador for Christ, a representative for the gospel, was in chains *but free.*

Undoubtedly, what upset the community at the time was revealing the mystery, the mystery that believing Jews and believing Gentiles are now formed into one new society: Under Christ as the head.

Paul gives a short personal greeting and encouragement in vv. 21-22. Tychicus had been an encouragement to Paul, now Paul encourages his readers by sending Tychicus to them. Each one of us can and should encourage one another.

He was sending Tychicus from Rome to Ephesus to update them on his situation. In addition, he commends him, ²¹ *Tychicus, the beloved brother and faithful minister in the Lord.*

There are five references to Tychicus in the New Testament:

1. He traveled with Paul from Greece to Asia (Acts 20:4)
2. He traveled *for* Paul as a messenger to church at Colossae (Colossians 4:7-8)
3. Paul sent him to Ephesus (in this verse)
4. He was with Timothy (2 Timothy 4:12)
5. With Titus (Titus 3:12)

Even though not well known today, he was certainly a faithful minister in *his* day. Paul's final greeting used his characteristic words: v. 23 *Peace, love, faith,* and v. 24 *Grace.*

Peace to God's family. Isn't that the way a letter should end? Every battle should end that way. Peace with God, with Christ, with self and with each other. The peaceful way of life was first on Paul's mind, and close behind is love; love *joined with faith.*

All the correct doctrine in the world meant nothing without love for Christ and each other.

The final comment from Paul:

> [24] *Grace be with all who love our Lord Jesus Christ with undying and incorruptible [love]. Amen (so let it be).*

This summarizes Paul's message of love in this letter.

- In 4:2 **Bear** with one another in love
- In 4:15, **Speak** the truth to one another in love
- **Build** up each other . . . . in love (4:16)
- **Walk** in love (5:2)
- **Love our spouses** with Christ's self-giving love (5:25, 28, 33)
- And **love Christ** (6:24)

Section Eight
Additional Questions and Thoughts for Discussion

1. How do you explain that a believer lives in a battleground?
2. How important are Paul's closing words *in conclusion?*
3. What are some of the devil's strategies and deceits? Discuss those mentioned by other members of the group.
4. List the hierarchy of Satan. How does the author list them as to rank?
5. From memory: What are the pieces of armor and what do each represent? What do you consider the most important? How does each piece help you?
6. What does the author suggest as the final piece of armament?
7. How has this study of the book of Ephesians helped you? Email any comments to the author.

ENDNOTES

1   Scripture taken from *The Expanded Bible*, Copyright © 2009 by Thomas Nelson, Inc. Used by permission. All rights reserved.

2   The *Emphasized Bible*, Copyright © 1994 by Kregel Publications, a division of Kregel, Inc., P.O. Box 2607, Grand Rapids, MI 49501. Used by permission.

3   Colossians, Philippians, Philemon.

4   Joseph Armitage Robinson (January 9, 1858-May 7, 1933) was a priest in the Church of England and scholar.

5   Sir Francis Bacon (1561-1626) was an English philosopher, statesman, scientist, lawyer, jurist and author.

6   In Christ.

7   Charles R. Swindoll, *The Living Insights Study Bible*, 1996, Zondervan, Grand Rapids, Michigan.

8   H.A. Ironside, The Exploring Series, *In the Heavenlies* (New York: Loizeaux Brothers, 1946).

9   *Advanced Foundations For A Living Faith,* Copyright © 2009, Thomas Hiegel, TLH Creations, Dayton OH.

10   Dr. Myles Munroe has published numerous books including: *Kingdom Principles* and *The Most Important Person on Earth.*

11   J. Vernon McGee, *Thru The Bible Series, Ephesians*, 1995, Thomas Nelson.

12   *The Hidden Man,* E.W. Kenyon, 1970, Kenyon's Gospel Publishing Society, Inc. Lynnwood, Washington.

13   Smith Wigglesworth (June 8, 1859-March 12, 1947), was a British evangelist who was important in the early history of Pentecostalism.

14   F.B. Meyer (Frederick Brotherton Meyer) 1847-1929 a contemporary and friend of D.L. Moody was a Baptist pastor and evangelist in England.

15   Dozens of other names and characteristics of the Devil taken from *Help From The Bible....When You Need It!* Thomas Hiegel, Copyright © 1996 by TLH Creations, Dayton, OH.

16 *The Battle in The Combat Zone of Our Mind,* a teaching course by Thomas L. Hiegel, 2011, TLH Creations, Dayton, OH

17 James Montgomery Boice, *Ephesians,* 1988, 1997, 2006 Baker Books, 58.

18 Rick Warren, *The Purpose Driven Life*, 2002, Zondervan, Grand Rapids, Michigan.

19 Kay Arthur, *His Imprint, My Expression*, 1993, Harvest House Pub.

20 *Travel Through the Old Testament* (in three volumes), Thomas Hiegel, Copyright © 2009 by TLH Creations, Dayton, OH.

21 Copied from Josephus, *The Jewish War and Jewish Antiquities.*

22 Mackay, *The Message of Ephesians,* p. 124.   Used by permission of Inter-Varsity Press-US and InterVarsity Press-UK.

23 John R. W. Stott, *God's New Society: The message of Ephesians* (Downers Grove, Ill.: InterVarsity, 1979).

24 Christians.

25 Taken from the brochure *From the Agony of the Cross, to the Triumph of the Throne*, Thomas Hiegel, Copyright © 2011, TLH Creations, Dayton OH.

26 William Barclay, *The Letters to the Galatians and Ephesians*, The Daily Study Bible Series (Philadelphia, Pa.; Westminster Press, 1976), 149.

27 Lee Strobel, *The Case for a Creator,* Copyright © 2004, Zondervan, Grand Rapids, Michigan.

28 Elizabeth George, *A Wife After God's Own Heart*, (Eugene, OR: Harvest House, 2004).

29 Rick Renner, *Sparkling Gems from the Greek,* Copyright © 2003 by Rick Renner, P.O. Box 702040, Tulsa, OK 74170-2040.